Y0-EKB-912

Adobe® Dreamweaver® CS3

Level 1

Adobe® Dreamweaver® CS3: Level 1

Part Number: 084204
Course Edition: 1.0

NOTICES

DISCLAIMER: While Element K Corporation takes care to ensure the accuracy and quality of these materials, we cannot guarantee their accuracy, and all materials are provided without any warranty whatsoever, including, but not limited to, the implied warranties of merchantability or fitness for a particular purpose. The name used in the data files for this course is that of a fictitious company. Any resemblance to current or future companies is purely coincidental. We do not believe we have used anyone's name in creating this course, but if we have, please notify us and we will change the name in the next revision of the course. Element K is an independent provider of integrated training solutions for individuals, businesses, educational institutions, and government agencies. Use of screenshots, photographs of another entity's products, or another entity's product name or service in this book is for editorial purposes only. No such use should be construed to imply sponsorship or endorsement of the book by, nor any affiliation of such entity with Element K. This courseware may contain links to sites on the Internet that are owned and operated by third parties (the "External Sites"). Element K is not responsible for the availability of, or the content located on or through, any External Site. Please contact Element K if you have any concerns regarding such links or External Sites.

TRADEMARK NOTICES Element K and the Element K logo are trademarks of Element K Corporation and its affiliates.

Adobe® Dreamweaver® CS3 is a registered trademark of Adobe Systems Incorporated in the U.S. and other countries; the Adobe products and services discussed or described may be trademarks of Adobe Systems Incorporated. All other product names and services used throughout this course may be common law or registered trademarks of their respective proprietors.

Copyright © 2007 Element K Corporation. All rights reserved. Screenshots used for illustrative purposes are the property of the software proprietor. This publication, or any part thereof, may not be reproduced or transmitted in any form or by any means, electronic or mechanical, including photocopying, recording, storage in an information retrieval system, or otherwise, without express written permission of Element K, 500 Canal View Boulevard, Rochester, NY 14623, (585) 240-7500, (800) 478-7788. Element K Courseware's World Wide Web site is located at **www.elementkcourseware.com**.

This book conveys no rights in the software or other products about which it was written; all use or licensing of such software or other products is the responsibility of the user according to terms and conditions of the owner. Do not make illegal copies of books or software. If you believe that this book, related materials, or any other Element K materials are being reproduced or transmitted without permission, please call (800) 478-7788.

HELP US IMPROVE OUR COURSEWARE

Your comments are important to us. Please contact us at Element K Press LLC, 1-800-478-7788, 500 Canal View Boulevard, Rochester, NY 14623, Attention: Product Planning, or through our Web site at **http://support.elementkcourseware.com**.

Adobe® Dreamweaver® CS3: Level 1

Lesson 6: Uploading a Website

Appendix A: Adobe Certified Expert (ACE) Program®

About This Course

You may want to make information available on the Internet. To achieve this, you need to create a website. In this course, you will design, build, and upload a website using Dreamweaver.

Creating web pages using HTML code can be a tedious task. It would be simpler if you can create web pages by the click of a few buttons. Dreamweaver provides you with features to easily create and upload websites.

Course Description

Target Student

Students who wish to familiarize themselves with the basic techniques used for creating websites using the Adobe Dreamweaver CS3 application. It also provides the fundamental knowledge and techniques needed to advance to more complex Dreamweaver operations for enhancing the functionality of websites.

Course Prerequisites

To ensure the successful completion of Adobe Dreamweaver CS3: Level 1, the student should have an understanding of how to use Microsoft Windows 2000 or Windows XP operating systems.

How to Use This Book

As a Learning Guide

Each lesson covers one broad topic or set of related topics. Lessons are arranged in order of increasing proficiency with *Adobe® Dreamweaver® CS3*; skills you acquire in one lesson are used and developed in subsequent lessons. For this reason, you should work through the lessons in sequence.

We organized each lesson into results-oriented topics. Topics include all the relevant and supporting information you need to master *Adobe® Dreamweaver® CS3*, and activities allow you to apply this information to practical hands-on examples.

You get to try out each new skill on a specially prepared sample file. This saves you typing time and allows you to concentrate on the skill at hand. Through the use of sample files, hands-on activities, illustrations that give you feedback at crucial steps, and supporting background information, this book provides you with the foundation and structure to learn *Adobe® Dreamweaver® CS3* quickly and easily.

As a Review Tool

Any method of instruction is only as effective as the time and effort you are willing to invest in it. In addition, some of the information that you learn in class may not be important to you immediately, but it may become important later on. For this reason, we encourage you to spend some time reviewing the topics and activities after the course. For additional challenge when reviewing activities, try the "What You Do" column before looking at the "How You Do It" column.

As a Reference

The organization and layout of the book make it easy to use as a learning tool and as an after-class reference. You can use this book as a first source for definitions of terms, background information on given topics, and summaries of procedures.

Course Icons

Icon	Description
	A **Caution Note** makes students aware of potential negative consequences of an action, setting, or decision that are not easily known.
	Display Slide provides a prompt to the instructor to display a specific slide. Display Slides are included in the Instructor Guide only.
	An **Instructor Note** is a comment to the instructor regarding delivery, classroom strategy, classroom tools, exceptions, and other special considerations. Instructor Notes are included in the Instructor Guide only.
	Notes Page indicates a page that has been left intentionally blank for students to write on.
	A **Student Note** provide additional information, guidance, or hints about a topic or task.
	A **Version Note** indicates information necessary for a specific version of software.

Certification

This course is designed to help you prepare for the following certification.

Certification Path: Adobe Certified Expert (ACE) Program®

Course Objectives

In this course, you will design, build, and upload a website.

You will:

- prepare to use the Dreamweaver environment.
- create a website.
- add design elements to web pages.
- work with links.
- work with frames.
- upload a website.

Course Requirements

Hardware

- An Intel® Pentium® IV processor.
- 512 MB of RAM.
- 1 GB of available disk space for software installation, and an additional 10 MB for the course data files.
- A 256-color monitor capable of 1024 x 768 resolution.
- A DVD-ROM drive.
- Internet connection.

Software

- Adobe® Dreamweaver® CS3.
- Microsoft® Internet Explorer® 6.0 or above.
- Netscape® Navigator 8.0.

Class Setup

1. Install Adobe Dreamweaver CS3. If you already have a full version of Adobe Dreamweaver CS3 installed on your computer, this course will run best if you uninstall and reinstall Dreamweaver to reset the application to the default settings. *Warning:* Uninstalling and reinstalling Dreamweaver will require you to re-enter the serial number of the program. If you do not have the serial number and installation CD available, do not uninstall.

If you are unable to uninstall/reinstall the program, you should remove the Marvin's Gardens Products site, if it exists. Launch Dreamweaver and choose **Site→Manage Sites.** In the **Manage Sites** dialog box, click the Marvin's Gardens Products site, if it is listed, and click **Remove.** Exit Dreamweaver.

2. Make sure that you have web browser software properly installed on your computer. It is preferable to have both Netscape Navigator and Microsoft Internet Explorer installed, since they are the two most popular browsers.

3. Make sure that file extensions are enabled. Open **My Computer.** Choose **Tools→Folder Options.** The **Folder Options** dialog box appears. Select the *View* tab, uncheck the **Hide extensions for known file types** check box, and click **OK.**

4. On the course CD-ROM, run the 084204dd.exe self-extracting file located within. This will install a folder named 084204Data on your C drive. This folder contains all the data files that you will use to complete this course.

5. In addition to the specific setup procedures needed for this class to run properly, you should also check the Element K Press product support website at **http:// support.elementkcourseware.com** for more information. Any updates about this course will be posted there.

List of Additional Files

Printed with each activity is a list of files students open to complete that activity. Many activities also require additional files that students do not open, but are needed to support the file(s) students are working with. These supporting files are included with the student data files on the course CD-ROM or data disk. Do not delete these files.

1 Getting Started with Dreamweaver

Lesson Time: 45 minutes

Lesson Objectives:

In this lesson, you will prepare to use the Dreamweaver environment.

You will:

- Examine the basic concepts of web designing.
- Explore the components of the Dreamweaver environment.
- Customize the workspace.

Introduction

Being a novice user of Dreamweaver, you may want to familiarize yourself with its basic features before beginning to create a website. In this lesson, you will prepare to use the Dreamweaver environment in an efficient manner.

Imagine using a computer without having a basic understanding of its components and operations. You may have to spend hours trying to accomplish a simple task. The same would be the case if you were to use Dreamweaver without understanding its components or their use.

TOPIC A

Examine the Basic Concepts of Web Designing

Designing a good website calls for adequate preparation. Before you begin to create a website, you need to understand what constitutes a website, and the underlying principles that govern its design. In this topic, you will examine the basic concepts of web designing.

Creating well-designed websites is as important as displaying accurate content on it. Understanding the basic concepts of web designing will help you create a website that is easily navigable, and contains information under relevant groupings.

Web Pages

Definition:

A *web page* is a document created using the HTML code. It is used to provide information to the user. It can be accessed using a browser. A web page can contain objects such as text or images. It can also contain links to these objects or other web pages.

Example:

Websites

A *website* is a collection of web pages. Typically, it consists of a home page that is linked to other pages through text or images. Each website is identified by a unique Uniform Resource Locator (URL).

The Uniform Resource Locator (URL)

A Uniform Resource Locator (URL) is an address that uniquely identifies a website on the Internet. The first part of the address indicates the protocol used to access the website, and the second part specifies the IP address or the domain name of the website's location.

Figure 1-1: A Uniform Resource Locator (URL) with the Protocol and IP.

The Protocol

A protocol refers to the set of rules that governs the exchange of information on the Internet. Hypertext Transfer Protocol (HTTP) is the standard protocol used to transfer and retrieve data from a web server.

The IP Address

Each computer that is connected to the Internet, whether part of a large network on a university campus or in someone's home office, uses a unique Internet Protocol (IP) address. This is a numeric address that helps identify the computer on the Internet.

The Domain Name

A domain name is the unique textual name that corresponds to the numeric IP address of a computer. It is the name used commonly to access the website on the Internet.

HTML

HyperText Markup Language *(HTML)* is a scripting language that is used to create web pages. It not only allows you to add the text that appears on the web page but also provides you with parameters that control the appearance of the web page. It also adds functionality to the web page.

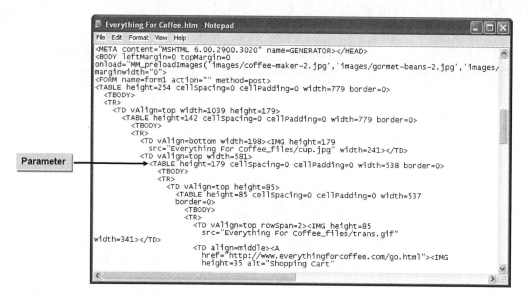

Figure 1-2: An HTML document.

The HTML Tags

HTML is made up of tags that act as code for creating the various elements, such as titles, tables, and ordered lists, of a web page. These HTML tags provide instruction to the web browser to display the elements on the page according to the values and attributes given to the tags.

The Website Access Process

A web server makes web pages accessible to users based on their request. This process consists of the following stages:

1. The user enters the URL of the website in the web browser.

2. The browser sends a request for the file to the web server through HTTP.

3. The web server sends the HTML text of the web page to the browser.

4. The browser reads the HTML text, formats the page according to the instructions provided in the HTML code, and displays it.

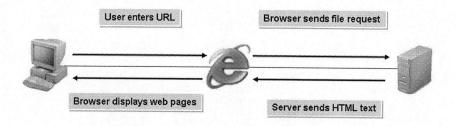

Figure 1-3: Image displaying the website access process.

Principles of Web Designing

Well-designed websites facilitate easy navigation through web pages for accessing the relevant information.

Guidelines

To develop a user-friendly website:

● Determine the purpose of the website.

   ■ What do you want the website to do?

   ■ Why are you creating the site?

   ■ Why will people come and visit the site?

● Identify the audience who will be visiting the site.

   ■ Are they new or experienced web surfers?

   ■ What kind of computer equipment will the site visitors have?

   ■ Will the visitors be savvy computer users?

   ■ What will the visitors want to do on the site?

● Organize the content for the website.

   ■ What topics or content will you have on the site?

   ■ Determine the content that can be grouped logically.

   ■ Frame a title for each of the groups.

   ■ Verify that there is flow of information across groups.

● Create a layout, an outline, or a site diagram that may make navigation easier and user friendly.

   ■ How will the information flow?

   ■ How will site visitors navigate through the site?

● Standardize the text format for the web page.

   ■ What text and background colors should be used?

   ■ What should be the font size of the headings and paragraph text?

   ■ What should be the font and font style of the text?

   ■ What is the paragraph format?

● Provide support for better user interactivity.

   ■ Provide meaningful file names for the web pages.

   ■ Provide information on the **About Us** and **Contact Us** pages, which will be helpful for the users.

   ■ Use the feedback and contact forms to get feedback from visitors.

Example:

Gardens is a local nursery with a loyal following of customers. The goal of the Gardens website is to increase customer loyalty by providing gardening information, and also to attract new customers. The target audience has been identified as predominantly homeowners. So, it is probably a good idea to design the site for modem connections, as opposed to high-speed connections. The site should also have a web page for providing contact details of Gardens so that users can contact the nursery and order the products.

ACTIVITY 1-1

Examining the Basic Concepts of Web Designing

Scenario:

You want to create a website that provides information about your company products. Before proceeding with the task, you want to ensure that you are thorough with the basic concepts of web designing.

---

1. **What does the first part of a URL indicate?**

    a) IP address

    b) Domain name

    c) File name

    d) Protocol

---

2. **Which statement is true about websites?**

    a) A website can contain only one web page.

    b) The web pages on a website cannot be linked through images.

    c) HTML can be used for creating web pages.

    d) Websites can contain information only in the form of text.

---

3. **True or False? Before creating a website, you need to identify the audience who will be visiting the site.**

    ___ True

    ___ False

TOPIC B
Explore the Dreamweaver Environment

Having examined the basic concepts of web designing, you are now ready to create a website using Dreamweaver. However, being a new user of the application, you may not be familiar with the functionality of the various components of its environment. In this topic, you will explore the Dreamweaver environment.

Working with the Dreamweaver application after knowing its environment thoroughly will help you finish the intended tasks in an efficient manner. Also, understanding the utilities of its various interface elements will enable you to make appropriate use of them.

The Dreamweaver Workspace

The Dreamweaver workspace consists of components that contain a variety of tools and commands for creating and enhancing web pages. The following table describes those components.

Component	Description
The Insert Bar	Contains tools for inserting objects, such as, tables, graphics, spry widgets, and hyperlinks that allow addition of a wide variety of details to pages.
The Document Toolbar	Contains options that help you perform tasks such as switching between different views, controlling the visual dynamics of a page, and checking web pages for accessibility standards.
The Status Bar	Contains components that help in selection of various page elements. It also provides information about the current page, such as the size and the magnification level of a document.
The Property Inspector	Contains options for modifying the properties of the various objects, such as text and graphics, placed on a web page. The options in this panel vary based on the object that is selected.
The Panel Groups	Contains a variety of panels grouped based on their functionality, such as managing files, editing HTML tags, adding dynamic content to pages, and tracking CSS rules and properties for pages. Each panel in a panel group appears as a tab.

Figure 1-4: *Components of the Dreamweaver workspace.*

Document Views

Dreamweaver allows you to work on a web page in three different views, namely the **Design, Code,** and **Split** views. The **Design** view displays a page the way it appears on the web browser, except that it is fully editable. The **Code** view displays the code used to create the page. The **Split** view displays both the design and code of the page in a single window.

The Guides Feature

Guides are lines that are used to position and align objects in a document. Guides also help you measure the sizes of page elements such as graphics. The **Lock Guides** option allows you to lock a guide so that it cannot be moved accidentally.

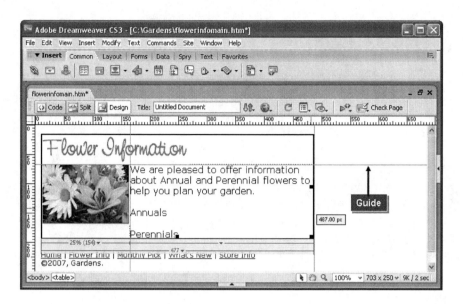

Figure 1-5: *A document with guides.*

ACTIVITY 1-2

Exploring the Dreamweaver Environment

Data Files:

index.htm

Scenario:

Now that you are thorough with the basic concepts of web designing, you want to start creating a website. You want to accomplish this task using the Dreamweaver application. However, you want to start your work only after familiarizing yourself with the different tools and options needed to create the web page.

What You Do	How You Do It
1. Open the **index.htm** file in the Dreamweaver CS3 application.	a. Choose **Start→All Programs→Adobe Dreamweaver CS3** to launch the Dreamweaver application.
	b. In the **Default Editor** dialog box, click **OK** to accept the default editing preferences.
	c. Choose **File→Open.**
	d. In the **Open** dialog box, navigate to the **C:\084204Data\Getting Started with Dreamweaver\Gardens** folder.
	e. Select **index.htm** and click **Open.**

2. **Which component in the Dreamweaver interface provides information about the size and the magnification level of a document?**

    a) The status bar

    b) The Insert bar

    c) The Property Inspector

    d) The Document toolbar

3. Explore the Dreamweaver interface.	a. In the **Files** panel group, select the **Assets** tab to view its options.

b. In the **CSS** panel group, click the
    expander arrow to expand the panel
    group.

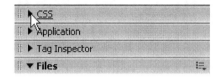

c. In the **CSS** panel group, click the
    expander arrow to collapse the panel
    group.

d. On the **Insert** bar, select the **Spry** tab to
    view the various tools it contains.

e. On the Document toolbar, click **Code** to
    view the document in the **Code** view.

f. Click **Split** to view the document in the
    Split view.

g. Click **Design** to return to the **Design** view.

4. **When would you use the Property Inspector?**

    a) To switch between the different views to view a document.

    b) To insert objects such as tables, graphics, spry widgets, and hyperlinks.

    c) To view the size of the current document.

    d) To modify the properties of objects such as text and graphics.

TOPIC C

Customize the Workspace

Having explored the various components of the Dreamweaver environment, you are ready to work with them. Before you begin, you may want to modify the default settings of the interface elements to suit your workflow and preferences. In this topic, you will customize the Dreamweaver workspace.

While creating a web page, you may have to use certain tools and commands more frequently. Making those tools and commands quickly accessible will help you work efficiently. Dreamweaver enables you to customize and save the workspace settings based on your work requirements.

Workspace Layouts

Dreamweaver provides three types of default workspace layouts that aid in designing web pages. The following table describes those workspace layouts.

Layout	Description
Coder	Displays the document window in **Code** view by default. It has the panel groups located on the left.
Designer	Integrates all document windows and panels into a single application window, with the panel groups located on the right.
Dual Screen	Useful in a two monitor setup. Displays the document window and the **Property Inspector** on the primary monitor, and all the panels on the secondary monitor.

The Preferences Dialog Box

The **Preferences** dialog box allows you to customize the Dreamweaver environment based on the work requirements. This dialog box contains several options grouped under different categories. These options allow you to perform tasks such as customizing the startup preferences, the browser settings, the functionality of codes, and the appearance of layout elements.

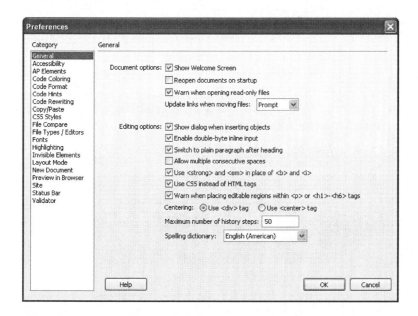

Figure 1-6: The Preferences dialog box displaying the options in the General category.

Categories in the Preferences Dialog Box

The **Preferences** dialog box contains a variety of customization options under different categories. The following table describes those categories.

Category	Description
General	Contains options for modifying the startup settings and editing preferences.
Accessibility	Contains options for prompting the user to add accessibility information for page elements, such as graphics and frames.
AP Elements	Contains options for modifying the default settings of the new AP elements the user creates.
Code Coloring	Contains options for setting color preferences for tags and code elements.
Code Format	Contains options for formatting code, such as casing of the tags, line length, and indentation for code.
Code Hints	Contains options for modifying the properties of code hints.
Code Rewriting	Contains options for specifying how Dreamweaver should rewrite code while modifying the properties of various elements.
Copy/Paste	Contains options for setting preferences for the Paste Special feature.
CSS Styles	Contains options for specifying how code that defines CSS styles need to be written.
File Compare	Contains options for comparing the code of remote and local versions of a document.
File Types / Editors	Contains options for specifying an external editor that edits files with specific extensions.

Category	Description
Fonts	Contains options for setting encoding preferences for fonts.
Highlighting	Contains options for customizing the colors that highlight library items, template regions, layout elements, third-party tags, and code in Dreamweaver.
Invisible Elements	Contains options for modifying the settings of icons that indicate invisible elements.
Layout Mode	Contains options for customizing the appearance of layout tables and cells.
New Document	Contains options for specifying which document type will be used as the default one for a website.
Preview in Browser	Contains options for modifying the settings of the browsers used for previewing a web page.
Site	Contains options for setting preferences for the file transfer features available in the **Files** panel.
Status Bar	Contains options for customizing the window sizes and connection speed displayed in the status bar.
Validator	Contains options for specifying the languages and problems against which the validator should check documents for errors.

How to Customize the Workspace

Procedure Reference: Hide a Panel

To hide a panel:

1. If necessary, in the desired panel group, click the **expander** arrow to expand the panel group.
2. In the desired panel group, from the **Options** menu, choose **Close panel group.**
3. If necessary, from the **Window** menu, select the panel/panel group name to restore the panel.

Procedure Reference: Dock a Panel

To dock a panel:

1. If necessary, from the **Window** menu, choose the desired panel to display it.
2. In the panel, click the gripper and drag it to the desired location
3. If necessary, click the gripper of the docked panel, and drag it to the desired location to undock the panel.

Gripper

Gripper refers to the vertical dotted lines located at the top-left corner of panel groups and toolbars. When you hover the mouse pointer over a gripper, the mouse pointer turns into a four-sided arrow; you can then drag the panel or toolbar to the desired location.

Procedure Reference: Group Panels

To group panels:

1. If necessary, in the desired panel group, click the **expander** arrow to expand the panel group.

2. Group the panels.

    ● In the panel group, from the **Options** menu, choose **Group <panel name> with** and choose the desired panel to group with.

    ● Or, click and drag the panel to the desired panel group.

Procedure Reference: Set Preferences

To set preferences:

1. Display the **Preferences** dialog box.

    ● Choose **Edit→Preferences.**

    ● Or, press **Ctrl+U.**

2. In the **Category** list box, select the desired category.

3. Specify the desired options.

4. Click **OK** to save the changes and close the **Preferences** dialog box.

Procedure Reference: Customize the Workspace

To customize the workspace:

1. Access the desired workspace layout.

    a. Choose **Window→Workspace Layout.**

    b. From the submenu displayed, choose the desired workspace layout.

2. Dock, hide, or group panels, and specify appropriate preferences.

3. Save the workspace.

    a. Choose **Window→Workspace Layout→Save Current.**

    b. In the **Save Workspace Layout** dialog box, in the **Name** text box, type the desired workspace name and click **OK.**

4. If necessary, delete a workspace layout.

    a. Choose **Window→Workspace Layout→Manage.**

    b. In the **Manage Workspace Layouts** dialog box, select the desired workspace layout and click **Delete.**

    c. In the **Adobe Dreamweaver CS3** dialog box, click **Yes** to delete the selected workspace layout.

    d. In the **Manage Workspace Layouts** dialog box, click **OK** to close the dialog box.

ACTIVITY 1-3

Customizing the Workspace

Before You Begin:

The index.htm file is open.

Scenario:

Before you start using Dreamweaver to create a web page, you would like to make some changes to the Dreamweaver interface so that you can arrange commands and options to suit your convenience.

What You Do	How You Do It
1. Explore the workspace layouts.	a. Choose **Window→Workspace Layout→ Coder** to apply the Coder layout to the interface.
	b. Observe that the Coder layout has panel groups docked to the left of the Dreamweaver window.
	c. Choose **Window→Workspace Layout→ Designer** to restore the Designer layout.
2. Customize the panel groups.	a. In the **Property Inspector,** from the **Options** menu, choose **Close panel group.**

	b. Observe that the **Property Inspector** is hidden.

c. In the **Files** panel, click the gripper and drag it to the document window until a black rectangle appears between the document window and the panel groups.

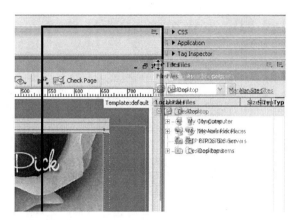

d. Observe that the **Files** panel group is docked between the document window and the panel groups.

e. In the **Application** panel group, click the **expander** arrow to expand the panel group.

f. Verify that the **Databases** panel is selected.

g. In the **Application** panel group, from the **Options** menu, choose **Group Databases with→Files.**

h. Observe that the **Databases** panel is now grouped with the panels in the **Files** panel group.

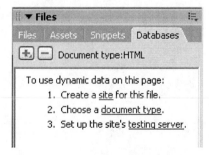

3. Set general preferences.

a. Choose **Edit→Preferences.**

b. In the **Preferences** dialog box, in the **Category** list box, verify that **General** is selected.

c. In the **Document options** section, uncheck the **Show Welcome Screen** check box to hide the welcome screen when the application is launched.

d. In the **Editing options** section, uncheck the **Show dialog when inserting objects** check box to be able to insert objects to web pages without being prompted for adding additional information.

e. Uncheck the **Use CSS instead of HTML tags** check box to use HTML tags to format web pages.

f. Click **OK** to save the changes.

4. Save the customized workspace.

a. Choose **Window→Workspace Layout→ Save Current.**

b. In the **Save Workspace Layout** dialog box, in the **Name** text box, type *My Layout*

c. Click **OK** to save the workspace layout.

Lesson 1 Follow-up

In this lesson, you prepared to use the Dreamweaver environment. As you are now familiar with the locations and utilities of the various tools and commands in the user interface, you will be able to get started with the work on your website with ease.

1. **For what kind of information would you create a website?**

2. **Of all the features available in Dreamweaver, which one will help you the most as you create websites? Why?**

2 | Creating a Website

Lesson Time: 1 hour(s), 25 minutes

Lesson Objectives:

In this lesson, you will create a website.

You will:

- Define a website.
- Create a web page.
- Format a web page.
- Organize files and folders.
- Create templates.

Introduction

You prepared yourself to use the Dreamweaver application. The next step would be to make use of its components to design web pages. In this lesson, you will create a website.

Given the growing popularity of the Internet, websites are considered as one of the powerful media for communication. Knowing how to create a website and work with its components will help you present information effectively to your site visitors.

TOPIC A
Define a Website

You customized the Dreamweaver environment to suit your work requirements. Now, you may need to group all the files you require to create the website in a common folder. In this topic, you will define a website.

Building a website calls for the usage of files of various types. When you have these files stored in a common location that is easily accessible, you need not waste time in navigating extensively to locate them. Thus, you will be able to create the web pages quickly and efficiently.

Site Definition

The **Site Definition** wizard is used to define a website. Using this wizard, you can name the website, specify its URL, and select its local root folder. When the site definition is complete, the **Files** panel will display all the files that are necessary for the operation of the site. These files include graphics, HTML files, and other objects.

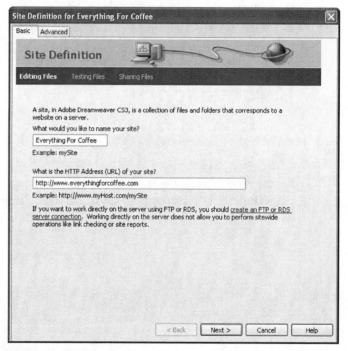

Figure 2-1: The Site Definition wizard.

The Case-Sensitive Link Checking Option
The **Site Definition** wizard contains an option for checking case-sensitive links. This option can be used to ensure that the case of the links matches with that of the file names when Dreamweaver checks the website links. However, this option is useful only on UNIX systems where the file names are case sensitive.

How to Define a Website

Procedure Reference: Define a New Website

To define a new website:

1. Choose **Site→New Site.**

2. In the **Site Definition** wizard, select the **Basic** tab.

3. In the **What would you like to name your site** text box, type the desired name and click **Next.**

4. Verify that the **No, I do not want to use a server technology** option is selected and click **Next.**

5. Verify that the **Edit local copies on my machine, then upload to server when ready (recommended)** option is selected and click the **Folder** icon.

6. In the **Choose local root folder for site <site name>** dialog box, navigate to the desired local root folder, which contains the files required to build the website, and click **Select.**

7. From the **How do you connect to your remote server** drop-down list, select **None** and click **Next.**

8. Click **Done** to define the site.

Procedure Reference: Change the Local Root Folder of a Defined Website

To change the local root folder of a defined website:

1. Choose **Site→Manage Sites.**

2. In the **Manage Sites** dialog box, select the desired website and click **Edit.**

3. In the **Site Definition** wizard, click **Next** twice.

4. Click the **Folder** icon, and in the **Choose local root folder for site <site name>** dialog box, navigate to the desired local root folder, which contains the files required to build the website.

5. Click **Select** to specify the local root folder.

6. In the **Site Definition** wizard, click **Next** twice and click **Done.**

7. In the **Adobe Dreamweaver CS3** message box, click **OK** to confirm the changes made to the site definition.

8. In the **Manage Sites** dialog box, click **Done** to apply the changes.

The Manage Sites Dialog Box

The **Manage Sites** dialog box is used for editing the definition of a website such as changing the location of the local root folder. It also allows you to create a new site, delete an existing site, and import or export a site's settings.

ACTIVITY 2-1

Defining a New Website

Before You Begin:

1. Choose **Edit→Preferences** to launch the **Preferences** dialog box.

2. In the **General** category, check the **Show Welcome Screen** and the **Show dialog when inserting objects** check boxes, and click **OK.**

3. Close the Dreamweaver application, and launch it again for the changes to reflect.

4. Choose **Window→Workspace Layout→Designer** to restore the Designer layout.

Scenario:

You are ready to create your company's website. You decide to start by making the files that are required to create the web pages quickly accessible.

What You Do	How You Do It
1. Specify the name for the new website.	a. Choose **Site→New Site** to launch the **Site Definition** wizard.
	b. On the **Basic** tab, in the **What would you like to name your site** text box, type *Gardens*
	c. Click **Next.**

2. Specify the settings for the site.

a. Verify that the **No, I do not want to use a server technology option** is selected and click **Next.**

b. Verify that the **Edit local copies on my machine, then upload to server when ready (recommended)** option is selected.

c. Click the **Folder** icon.

d. In the **Choose local root folder for site Gardens** dialog box, navigate to the **C:\084204Data\Creating a Website\ MyGardens** folder.

e. Click **Select** to specify the local root folder.

f. Click **Next.**

g. From the **How do you connect to your remote server** drop-down list, select **None** and click **Next.**

h. Verify that the summary of the settings you specified is displayed, and click **Done** to define the site.

i. If necessary, in the **Files** panel, to the left of the **Site - Gardens** folder, click the Plus Sign (+) to expand it.

j. Observe that the contents of the **MyGardens** folder are displayed.

ACTIVITY 2-2

Changing the Local Root Folder of a Defined Website

Scenario:

You want to redesign your web pages based on the changes made to the catalog of your company's products. Implementing those changes would mean, starting work on the website with a different set of HTML files and graphics. And, you want to be able to access those files quickly as you build the website.

What You Do	How You Do It
1. Launch the **Site Definition** wizard.	a. Choose **Site→Manage Sites.**
	b. In the **Manage Sites** dialog box, verify that **Gardens** is selected, and click **Edit** to launch the **Site Definition** wizard.

2. Change the location of the local root folder for the site.

a. In the **Site Definition** wizard, click **Next** two times.

b. Click the **Folder** icon.

c. In the **Choose local root folder for site Gardens** dialog box, navigate to the **C:\084204Data\Creating a Website\ Gardens** folder.

d. Click **Select** to specify the local root folder.

e. In the **Site Definition** wizard, click **Next** two times.

f. Click **Done.**

g. In the **Adobe Dreamweaver CS3** message box, click **OK** to confirm the changes made to the site definition.

h. In the **Manage Sites** dialog box, click **Done** to apply the changes.

i. If necessary, in the **Files** panel, to the left of the **Site - Gardens** folder, click the Plus Sign (**+**) to expand it.

j. Observe that the **Files** panel now displays the contents of the **Gardens** folder.

TOPIC B
Create a Web Page

You have defined a website, thereby making the files required to build the website easily accessible. The next step would be to start creating the elements that constitute a website. In this topic, you will create a web page.

The main purpose of creating a website is to display information. Knowing how to create web pages will help you present information in the appropriate format.

The New Document Dialog Box

The **New Document** dialog box contains categories based on which you can create different types of documents. The following table describes those categories.

Category	Description
Blank Page	Used to create blank web pages of various types, such as HTML, Javascript, and Coldfusion. It also allows you to select predefined CSS layouts for the pages.
Blank Template	Used to create templates of various types with predefined CSS layouts.
Page from Template	Used to create web pages based on existing templates.
Page from Sample	Used to create web pages based on sample pages that contain predefined elements, such as CSS style sheets, framesets, and themes.
Other	Used to create various types of pages, such as C#, Java, and VB Script pages.

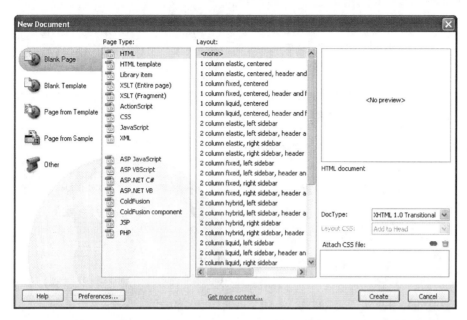

Figure 2-2: *The New Document dialog box displaying the page types in the Blank Page category.*

File Naming Conventions

While naming files, it is better to use lowercase characters without any spaces, punctuations, and special characters between them. This is because some web servers such as UNIX and LINUX are case sensitive and do not support special characters and punctuations. When you need to separate words in a file name, use an underscore or a hyphen.

The Home Page

The *home page* is the entry point of a website. It provides access to the other pages on the site. By default, it is named as index.htm. If the home page of the website is called home.htm, then it can be accessed only by typing home.htm, along with the URL of the site. Instead, if the home page is named as index.htm, you only need to type the URL of that site.

Page Size Resolution

Page size resolution refers to the number of individual pixels that a predetermined area or space in a page can contain. A page size of 800 x 600 denotes that 800 pixels are displayed horizontally and 600 pixels are displayed vertically. The higher the resolution, the smaller the screen elements will appear. When a web page with low resolution is viewed on a screen with higher resolution, the screen will display empty or white spaces.

Dreamweaver Extensions

Dreamweaver extensions refer to software that can be added to the Dreamweaver application to enhance its capabilities. Some of these extensions allow for reformatting of tables, writing a script for a browser, or connecting to back-end databases. Using the Extension Manager feature, you can install or delete Dreamweaver extensions.

How to Create a Web Page

Procedure Reference: Create a Web Page

To create a web page:

1. Choose **File→New.**
2. In the **New Document** dialog box, specify the desired page type.
3. Click **Create** to create the web page.
4. In the document window, add the desired content.
5. Choose **File→Save.**
6. In the **Save As** dialog box, navigate to the desired folder.
7. In the **File name** text box, click and type the desired file name.
8. Click **Save** to save the web page.

ACTIVITY 2-3
Creating a Web Page

Scenario:
As the first step towards creating the website, you decide to first get the basic information about the company ready for display.

What You Do	How You Do It
1. Create a blank web page.	a. Choose **File→New**.
	b. In the **New Document** dialog box, verify that the **Blank Page** category is selected.
	c. In the **Page Type** list box, verify that **HTML** is selected.
	d. Click **Create** to create a blank HTML document.

2. Enter text on the web page.

a. In the document window, type **Gardens** and press **Enter.**

b. Type **715 Vidalia Boulevard** and press **Enter.**

c. Type **Atlanta, GA 30018** and press **Enter.**

d. Type **(717) 555–1444** and press **Enter.**

e. Type **Store Hours** and press **Enter.**

f. Type **Mon-Sat 7am-9pm** and press **Enter.**

g. Type **Sun 8am-6pm** and press **Enter.**

h. Type **Directions**

3. Save the web page.

   a. Choose **File→Save.**

   b. If necessary, in the **Save As** dialog box, navigate to the **C:\084204Data\Creating a Website\Gardens** folder.

   c. In the **File name** text box, click and type *store.htm*

   d. Click **Save** to save the web page.

TOPIC C
Format a Web Page

You have created a web page. You may now want to enhance its appearance. In this topic, you will format a web page.

On the web page you create, you may want to direct the user's attention to specific details. Or, you may want to break the monotony across the various pages of textual content on your website. The various formatting options available in Dreamweaver will help you present attractive and legible content to your site visitors.

Text Properties

The appearance of text on a web page is controlled by the properties of the text, such as its font type, size, color, paragraph format, style, alignment, and indenting. You can either use the **Property Inspector,** or the **Text** menu to modify these properties.

The Page Properties Dialog Box

The **Page Properties** dialog box is used to modify the settings of an entire web page. Using this dialog box, you can modify the text properties, margin styles, the background color, and the background image of a page. It also allows you to give a title to the web page.

Lists

Lists are used to display content in a structured format. Dreamweaver provides three types of lists, namely unordered, ordered, and definition lists. In an unordered list, each list item is preceded by a bullet. In an ordered list, each list item is preceded by a number. In a definition list, alternate paragraphs are formatted as a term or related definition.

How to Format a Web Page

Procedure Reference: Remove Paragraph Breaks Between Text

To remove paragraph breaks between text:
1. Click to the left of the text for which you want to remove the paragraph break.
2. Press **Backspace.**
3. Hold down **Shift** and press **Enter** to remove the paragraph break.

Procedure Reference: Format Text on a Web Page

To format text on a web page:
1. Select the desired text.
   - Click and drag to select the desired text.
   - Or, click before the text, hold down **Shift,** and click after the text.
2. Format the text.
   - Change the paragraph format of the text.
     - In the **Property Inspector,** from the **Format** drop-down list, select the desired format.

- Or, choose **Text→Paragraph Format** and from the **Paragraph Format** submenu, choose the desired format.
- Change the font of the text.
  - In the **Property Inspector,** from the **Font** drop-down list, select the desired font.
  - Or, choose **Text→Font** and from the **Font** submenu, choose the desired font.
- Change the size of the text.
  - In the **Property Inspector,** from the **Size** drop-down list, select the desired font size.
  - Or, choose **Text→Size** and from the **Size** submenu, choose the desired size.
- Change the style of the text.
  - In the **Property Inspector,** click the **Bold** button, or the **Italic** button.
  - Or, choose **Text→Style** and from the **Style** submenu, choose the desired style.
- Change the color of the text.
  - In the **Property Inspector,** click the **Text Color** button and choose the desired color.
  - Or, next to the **Text Color** button, click in the text box, type the desired value, and press **Enter.**
- Indent the text.
  - In the **Property Inspector,** click the **Text Indent** button.
  - Or, choose **Text→Indent.**

Procedure Reference: Change the Background Color of a Web Page

To change the background color of a web page:

1. Choose **Modify→Page Properties.**
2. In the **Page Properties** dialog box, in the **Category** list box, select **Appearance.**
3. Specify the desired back ground color for the page.
   - Click the **Background Color** button and choose the desired color.
   - Or, in the **Background Color** text box, type the desired value.
4. Click **OK** to apply the changes.

Procedure Reference: Specify a Title for a Web Page Using the Page Properties Dialog Box

To specify a title for a web page using the **Page Properties** dialog box:

1. Choose **Modify→Page Properties.**
2. In the **Page Properties** dialog box, in the **Category** list box, select **Title/Encoding.**
3. In the **Title** text box, type the desired name.
4. Click **OK.**

Procedure Reference: Specify a Title for a Web Page Using the Document Toolbar

To specify a title for a web page using the Document toolbar:

1. On the Document toolbar, in the Title text box, select the text Untitled Document.

2. Type the desired text to give a title to the document.

Procedure Reference: Format a List

To format a list:

1. Select the text that you want to format as a list.
2. Format the selected text.
   - Format the text as an ordered list.
     - In the **Property Inspector,** click the **Ordered List** button.
     - Or, choose **Text→List→Ordered List.**
   - Format the text as an unordered list.
     - In the **Property Inspector,** click the **Unordered List** button.
     - Or, choose **Text→List→Unordered List.**
   - Choose **Text→List→Definition List** to format the text as a definition list.

Procedure Reference: Preview a Web Page

To preview a web page:

1. Open the desired web page.
2. Preview the web page in the installed browser application.
   - Choose **File→Preview in Browser→<Installed Browser Application>.**
   - Or, on the Document toolbar, click the **Preview/Debug in Browser** button and choose **<Installed Browser Application>.**

ACTIVITY 2-4
Formatting Web Pages

Data Files:

store.htm, iristext.htm

Before You Begin:
The store.htm file is open.

Scenario:
You have entered the required content on your web pages. While reviewing them, you think that the appearance of the text is not appealing enough.

What You Do	How You Do It
1. Remove the unnecessary paragraph breaks between text.	a. Click to the left of the word **Atlanta** and press **Backspace**.
	b. Hold down **Shift** and press **Enter** to remove the paragraph break.

	c. Remove the paragraph break between the text **Mon-Sat 7am-9pm** and **Sun 8am-6pm**.
2. Format the text.	a. Click to the left of the text **Store Hours**.
	b. In the **Property Inspector,** from the **Format** drop-down list, select **Heading 2.**
	c. Click to the left of the word **Directions**.

d. Choose **Text→Paragraph Format→ Heading 2.**

Gardens

715 Vidalia Boulevard
Atlanta, GA 30018

(717) 555-1444

Store Hours

Mon-Sat 7am-9pm
Sun 8am-6pm

Directions

e. Click before the word **Gardens,** hold down **Shift,** and click at the end of the word to select the word.

f. In the **Property Inspector,** click the **Bold** button. **B**

g. From the **Font** drop-down list, select **Verdana, Arial, Helvetica, sans-serif.**

h. Next to the **Text Color** button, click in the text box, type *#000099* and press **Enter** to change the color of the text.

i. Click after the word **Gardens** to deselect the text.

j. Observe that the word **Gardens** reflects the formatting applied to it.

Gardens

715 Vidalia Boulevard
Atlanta, GA 30018

(717) 555-1444

---

3. Set page properties.

a. Choose **Modify→Page Properties.**

b. In the **Page Properties** dialog box, in the **Category** list box, select **Title/Encoding.**

c. In the **Title** text box, select the text **Untitled Document.**

d. Type *Store Information - Gardens* to specify the title for the web page.

e. In the **Category** list box, select **Appearance.**

f. In the **Background Color** text box, click and type *#669900*

g. Click **OK** to apply the changes.

---

4. Preview the web page on a browser.

a. Choose **File→Save.**

b. Choose **File→Preview in Browser→ IExplore** to preview the web page in Internet Explorer.

c. Close the Internet Explorer window.

---

5. Format a list.

a. Double-click **iristext.htm** to open the file.

b. In the document window, click before the word **Bearded.**

c. Scroll down to view the word **Bulb.**

d. Hold down **Shift** and click after the word **Bulb.**

e. In the **Property Inspector,** click the **Unordered List** button. ▤

f. Observe that the selected text is formatted as an unordered list.

g. Click before the words **Miniature dwarf.**

h. Hold down **Shift** and click after the word **Border.**

i. In the **Property Inspector,** click the **Text Indent** button, ▤ to indent the selected text.

j. In the document window, click anywhere to deselect the text.

Types

- Bearded
  - Miniature dwarf
  - Standard dwarf
  - Miniature tall
  - Intermediate
  - Border
- Beardless
- Crested
- Bulb

k. Save the web page.

l. Choose **File→Close All** to close all the documents.

TOPIC D
Organize Files and Folders

You formatted the web pages on your website. You may now want to place the files that you frequently work with in a separate folder so that they can be easily identified. In this topic, you will organize files and folders using the **Files** panel.

While working on multiple files in a single folder, locating a particular file could be difficult. By organizing these files into different folders according to the work flow, you will be able to access them easily. Also, grouping files based on their development status will help you distinguish the files that you are currently working with from the rest.

How to Organize Files and Folders

Procedure Reference: Create a New Folder

To create a new folder:

1. If necessary, in the **Files** panel, click the **Expand to show local and remote sites** button.
2. In the **Files** panel, select the folder in which you want to create a new folder.
3. If necessary, to the left of the selected folder, click the Plus Sign (+) to view the files within it.
4. If necessary, to the left of the selected folder, click the Minus Sign (-) to collapse it.
5. Create a folder.
   - In the **Files** panel, right-click the folder and choose **New Folder.**
   - In the **Files** panel group, from the **Options** menu, choose **File→New Folder.**
   - Or, press **Ctrl+Alt+Shift+N.**
6. Type a name for the new folder and press **Enter.**

Procedure Reference: Create a New File

To create a new file:

1. In the **Files** panel, select the folder in which you want to create a new file.
2. Create a file.
   - In the **Files** panel, right-click the folder and choose **New File.**
   - In the **Files** panel group, from the **Options** menu, choose **File→New File.**
   - Or, press **Ctrl+Alt+N.**
3. Type a name for the new file and press **Enter.**

Procedure Reference: Move Files into a Folder

To move files into a folder:

1. In the **Files** panel, select the file that you want to move into a folder.
2. If necessary, hold down **Ctrl** and select the other files.
3. Drag the selected files into the desired folder.
4. In the **Update Files** dialog box, click **Update** to update the links to the moved files.

ACTIVITY 2-5

Organizing Files and Folders

Data Files:

index.htm

Scenario:

As you build your website, you notice that the number of files used on the website has increased. You are now finding it difficult to locate the files that require development.

What You Do	How You Do It
1. View the contents of the **Graphics** folder.	a. In the **Files** panel, click the **Expand to show local and remote sites** button.
	b. In the right pane, to the left of the **Graphics** folder, click the Plus Sign (**+**) to view the files within it.
	c. To the left of the **Graphics** folder, click the Minus Sign (**-**) to collapse it.
2. Create a new folder.	a. Choose **File→New Folder** to create a new folder.
	b. Type *Working* and press **Enter.**
3. Move the files under development into the **Working** folder.	a. In the right pane, select the **iristext.htm** file and drag it to the **Working** folder.
	b. In the **Update Files** dialog box, click **Update** to update the links to those files.
	c. In the right pane, select the **homepagetext.htm** file, hold down **Ctrl,** and select the **pricestart.htm** file.
	d. Drag the selected files to the **Working** folder.
	e. In the **Update Files** dialog box, click **Update** to update the links to the files.

TOPIC E
Create Templates

You created web pages. You may now want to ensure consistency in the look and feel of all the pages on your site. In this topic, you will create templates.

Sometimes, you may want certain information to appear consistently on all the pages of your website. Entering the information in each of the pages can be cumbersome and time consuming. Being able to work with Dreamweaver templates minimizes the effort spent on creating web pages with similar formats.

Templates

Definition:

A *template* is a document that contains predefined design elements, such as graphics and text. It can also contain functional settings such as links. Using a template, you can create several web pages that share common design elements. Templates can be modified according to your preferences.

Example:

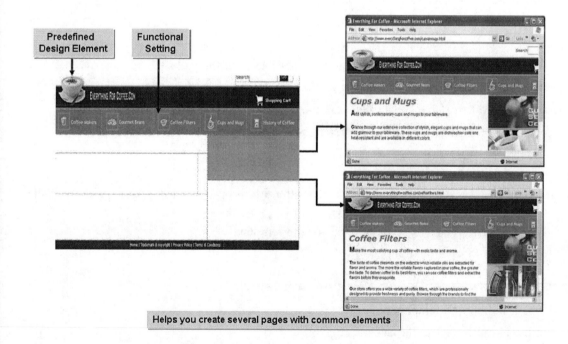

Helps you create several pages with common elements

Limitation of Templates

Templates cannot be used to store elements that you may want to use in a variety of combinations or in different places on each page.

Regions of a Template

In Dreamweaver templates, you can define regions that aid in the development of web pages. The following table describes those regions.

Region	Description
Non-editable	This region remains locked and therefore the elements in it cannot be modified. By default, the entire area in a template is non-editable.
Editable	This region contains elements that can be modified according to the user's preferences.
Repeating	This region can be replicated any number of times based on the user's preferences.
Optional	This region can be shown or hidden according to the user's preferences.

How to Create Templates

Procedure Reference: Create a Template

To create a template:

1. Create a new web page.
2. Add the content that is to be replicated across pages on the website.
3. If necessary, add a special character to the template.
    a. On the **Insert** bar, select the **Text** tab.
    b. On the **Text** tab, click the **Characters** button and choose the desired special character.
4. Choose **File→Save As Template.**
5. In the **Save As Template** dialog box, from the **Site** drop-down list, select the desired site in which the template has to be saved.
6. In the **Save As** text box, type a name for the template.
7. Click **Save** to save the template.

Procedure Reference: Define a Region in a Template

To define a region in a template:

1. In the template, select the desired region.
2. Define the selected region.
    - Choose **Insert→Template Objects→Editable Region** to define the region as an editable region.
    - Choose **Insert→Template Objects→Optional Region** to define the region as an optional region.
    - Choose **Insert→Template Objects→Repeating Region** to define the region as a repeating region.

Procedure Reference: Create a Page from a Template

To create a page from a template:

1. Choose **File→New.**
2. In the **New Document** dialog box, select the **Page from Template** category.
3. In the **Site** list box, select the site that contains the template based on which you want to create a web page.
4. In the **Template for Site "<Site Name>"** list box, select the desired template.
5. Click **Create** to create a page based on the template.

Procedure Reference: Apply a Template to a Web Page

To apply a template to a web page:

1. Open the web page to which you want to apply a template.
2. In the **Files** panel group, select the **Assets** tab.
3. In the **Assets** panel, on the left side, click the **Templates** button.
4. In the **Name** list box, select the desired template.
5. At the bottom of the **Assets** panel, click **Apply** to apply the selected template to the page.
6. If necessary, specify the region on the template to which you want to move the required content of the web page.
   a. In the **Inconsistent Region Names** dialog box, in the **Name** list box, select the desired region of the web page.
   b. From the **Move content to new region** drop-down list, select the region of the template in which you want the selected content to appear.
   c. Click **OK.**

Procedure Reference: Modify a Template

To modify a template:

1. Open the desired template.
2. Make the desired changes to the template.
3. Choose **File→Save.**
4. In the **Update Template Files** dialog box, click **Update** to reflect the changes on all the web pages that were created based on this template.
5. In the **Update Pages** dialog box, click **Close.**

ACTIVITY 2-6

Creating a Template

Data Files:

index.htm

Before You Begin:

In the **Files** panel, click the **Collapse to show local and remote sites** button to collapse the panel.

Scenario:

You want to create a web page that contains the copyright information of the company. You want this information to appear consistently on all the pages on the website.

What You Do	How You Do It
1. Create an HTML page with the copyright information.	a. Choose **File→New.**
	b. Click **Create** to create a blank HTML document.
	c. Choose **Modify→Page Properties** to launch the **Page Properties** dialog box.
	d. In the **Appearance** section, in the **Background Color** text box, click and type *#669900*
	e. In the **Page Properties** dialog box, click **OK** to apply the changes.
	f. Press **Enter.**
	g. On the **Insert** bar, select the **Text** tab.
	h. On the **Text** tab, click the **Characters** button and select **Copyright** to insert the copyright symbol on the web page.
	i. In the document window, type *2007, Gardens*
	j. Hold down **Shift** and click before the © symbol to select the text.
	k. In the **Property Inspector,** from the **Font** drop-down list, select **Verdana, Arial, Helvetica, sans-serif.**
	l. From the **Size** drop-down list, select **4.**
	m. Click at the end of the word **Gardens** to deselect the text.
2. Save the page as a template.	a. Choose **File→Save as Template.**
	b. In the **Save As Template** dialog box, in the **Save As** text box, type *default*
	c. Click **Save** to save the web page as a template.

3. Define the editable region in the template.

a. In the document window, verify that the insertion point is placed at the top-left corner.

b. Choose **Insert→Template Objects→ Editable Region.**

c. In the **New Editable Region** dialog box, in the **Name** text box, type *main text* to specify a name for the editable region.

d. Click **OK.**

e. In the document window, observe that an editable region has been defined.

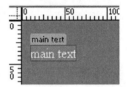

f. In the editable region, click before the word **main.**

g. Hold down **Shift** and click outside the border surrounding the editable region to select the entire text.

h. In the **Property Inspector,** from the **Font** drop-down list, select **Verdana, Arial, Helvetica, sans-serif.**

i. In the document window, click after the word **text** to deselect the text.

j. Choose **File→Save** to save the default.dwt template.

k. In the document window, click the **Close** button to close the default.dwt template.

4. Create a web page based on the template.

a. Choose **File→New.**

b. In the **New Document** dialog box, select the **Page from Template** category.

c. In the **Site** list box, verify that **Gardens** is selected.

d. In the **Templates for Site "Gardens"** list box, verify that **default** is selected, and click **Create.**

e. On the Document toolbar, in the **Title** text box, select the text **Untitled Document.**

f. Type *What's New - Gardens* to give a title to the document.

g. Save the web page as *whatsnew.htm* in the **C:\084204Data\Creating a Website\ Gardens** folder.

h. In the document window, click the **Close** button to close the whatsnew.htm file.

5. Apply the default template to the **flowerinfomain.htm** page.

a. In the **Files** panel, double click the **flowerinfomain.htm** file to open it.

b. In the **Files** panel group, select the **Assets** tab.

c. In the **Assets** panel, on the left side, click the **Templates** button.

d. In the **Name** list box, verify that the **default** template is selected.

e. At the bottom of the **Assets** panel, click **Apply.**

f. In the **Inconsistent Region Names** dialog box, in the **Name** list box, select **Document body.**

g. From the **Move content to new region** drop-down list, select **main text.**

h. Click **OK** to apply the template to the page.

i. Choose **File→Save** to save the flowerinfomain.htm file.

j. In the document window, click the **Close** button to close the flowerinfomain.htm file.

Lesson 2 Follow-up

In this lesson, you defined a website, created web pages, organized site files, and created templates. You will now be able to present information effectively to your site visitors.

1. **When would you create web pages using templates?**

2. **What type of formatting would you apply to your web pages to make them look more appealing? Why?**

3 | Adding Design Elements to Web Pages

Lesson Time: 1 hour(s), 15 minutes

Lesson Objectives:

In this lesson, you will add design elements to web pages.

You will:

- Insert images.
- Insert tables.
- Create repeating region templates.

Introduction

You have created basic web pages. You may now need to ensure that the information presented on the website is clearly comprehended by the user. In this lesson, you will add design elements to web pages.

Information can be presented in more than one way to the user. By using the design elements that best suit your content, you would be able to present information clearly to the users.

TOPIC A
Insert Images

You have created and formatted a basic web page. Now, you may want to make it look more attractive. In this topic, you will insert images.

A web page that contains only textual content might not interest a user. By adding images, you can make the web page visually appealing. It also would illustrate the site's content clearly to the user.

Image Properties

Image properties allow you to specify how images are displayed on a web page. Some of the common image properties are width, height, spacing, alignment, and alternate text.

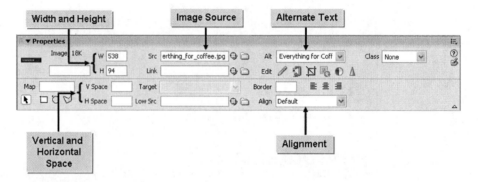

Figure 3-1: Properties of an image.

Use of Alternate Text

If an HTML page contains images, the text on the page downloads before the images do. Placeholders indicating the presence of an image appear on the page while the images are loading. Placeholders also appear if the viewer has turned off the option of automatic image loading, as it sometimes happens when the connection is very slow. In such instances, the alternate text that appears in the image placeholder gives a description of the image. It also appears when you move the mouse pointer over an image, but only certain browsers support it.

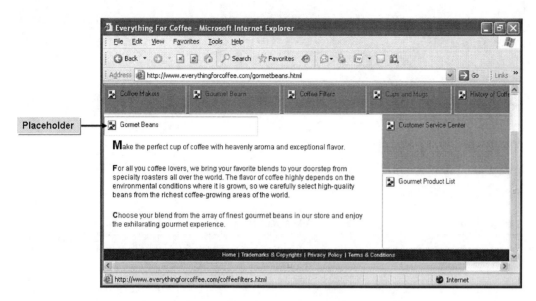

Figure 3-2: *A web page with placeholder.*

Graphic File Formats for the Web

There are three graphic file formats that are commonly used on web pages. The following table describes these formats.

File Format	Description
Graphic Interchange Format (GIF)	Limited to 256 colors and therefore is most useful for images with few colors or with large areas of flat colors. You can reduce the file size of GIF images by reducing the number of colors within the image. GIF images also support transparency; so, page background can be made visible through portions of the image.
Joint Photographic Experts Group (JPEG)	Uses compression to dramatically reduce the file size, thus allowing for faster download and display. When the compression level in a JPEG image is increased, the file size as well as the quality is reduced. JPEG images are best suited for photographs and other images that contain more than 256 colors.
Portable Network Graphic (PNG)	Supports more than 256 colors, along with transparency. Since PNG is the native graphics format for Adobe Fireworks, when you use it in Dreamweaver, you can maintain layers, transparency, and other graphics information in the original file. PNG also offers compression, but it does not reduce image size like JPEG does.

JPEG images do not support transparency. So, the background of your image should match with that of the web page to avoid a visible rectangular area around the image when viewed.

Alignment Options

The **Align** drop-down list in the **Property Inspector** provides several alignment options for aligning the images on a web page.

The following table describes the alignment options.

Alignment Option	Description
Default	This uses the browser's default alignment.
Baseline	The bottom of the image is aligned with the baseline of the surrounding text.
Top	The top of the image is aligned with the top of the tallest object in the current line.
Middle	The middle of the image is aligned with the baseline of the current line.
Bottom	The bottom of the image is aligned with the baseline of the text in the current line.
Text Top	The top of the image is aligned with the tallest character in the current line of the text.
Absolute Middle	The middle of the image is aligned with the middle of the text or object in the current line.
Absolute Bottom	The bottom of the image is aligned with the descenders in the current line of text.
Left or **Right**	The image is aligned to the left or right edge of the browser window or table cell, and the text in the current line flows around the left or right side of the image.

How to Insert Images

Procedure Reference: Insert an Image on a Page

To insert an image on a page:

1. Click in the desired location to place the insertion point.
2. Display the **Select Image Source** dialog box.
   - Choose **Insert→Image.**
   - Or, on the **Insert** bar, on the **Common** tab, click the **Images** button and select **Image.**
3. Navigate to the desired folder, select a file, and click **OK.**
4. In the **Image Tag Accessibility Attributes** dialog box, in the **Alternate Text** text box, type an alternate name for the image and click **OK.**

Procedure Reference: Set Image Properties

To set image properties:

1. Select the image.
2. In the **Property Inspector,** set the desired image properties.
   - Click in the **Width** text box and type a value to set the width of the image.
   - Click in the **Height** text box and type a value to set the height of the image.
   - Click in the **H Space** text box and type a value for horizontal space.
   - Click in the **V Space** text box and type a value for vertical space.
   - From the **Align** drop-down list, select the desired alignment option for the image.
   - Click in the **Alt** text box and type an alternate name for the image.
   - Click in the **Src** text box and modify the source of the image.

ACTIVITY 3-1

Inserting Images

Data Files:

iristext.htm

Before You Begin:

1. If you are starting the course with the lesson "Adding Design Elements to Web Pages", and the Gardens site was not previously defined in Dreamweaver, you must first define it by following the instructions in the activity "Defining a New Website", which is present in the lesson "Creating a Website", using the data from the C:\084204Data\Adding Design Elements to Web Pages\Gardens folder.

2. If the Gardens site was previously defined in Dreamweaver, you must modify it by following the instructions in the activity "Changing the Local Root Folder of a Defined Website", which is present in the lesson "Creating a Website", using the data from the C:\084204Data\Adding Design Elements to Web Pages\Gardens folder.

Scenario:

You have a web page with information about the Iris flower. You want to complement the text with an image of the Iris flower. You also need to ensure that the content is properly aligned.

What You Do	How You Do It
1. Add an image to the page.	a. Expand the **Site - Gardens** folder.
	b. Expand the **Working** folder.

	c. Double-click the **iristext.htm** file.
	d. Click before the word **Irises** and choose **Insert→Image.**
	e. In the **Select Image Source** dialog box, navigate to the **C:\084204Data\Adding Design Elements to Web Pages\ Gardens\Graphics** folder.
	f. Select the **iris46.jpg** file and click **OK.**

g. In the **Image Tag Accessibility Attributes** dialog box, in the **Alternate Text** text box, type *Iris* and click **OK.**

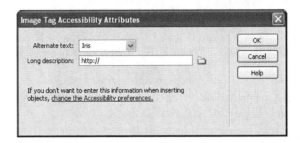

2. Specify the properties of the image.

a. In the **Property Inspector,** click in the **H Space** text box, type *10* and press **Enter.**

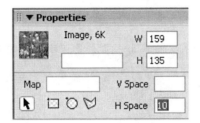

b. In the **Property Inspector,** from the **Align** drop-down list, select **Left.**

c. Save and close the file.

TOPIC B

Insert Tables

You have inserted images on a web page. Now, you may need to present content in an organized way. In this topic, you will insert tables.

When building simple pages, you have seen that it can be difficult to place elements onto the page where you want them. By using tables, you will be able to exactly position the elements on a page.

Tables

Tables allow you to organize data in grids of rows and columns. You can also use tables to create a layout for a web page. This helps to maintain the consistent appearance of text and images on a web page.

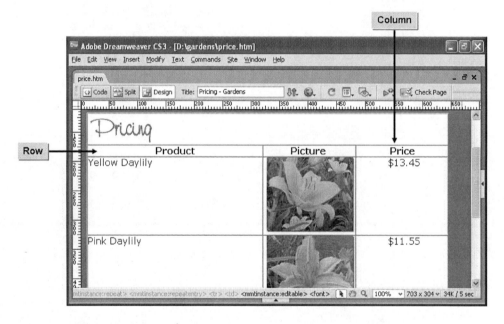

Figure 3-3: A table on a web page.

The <table> Tag

The <table> tag is used to create tables. Each table tag can contain multiple <tr> tags, which represent a table row, and each <tr> tag can contain multiple <td> tags, which represent the table cells.

Table Properties

The **Table** dialog box provides several options to specify table attributes.

The following table describes the options in the **Table** dialog box.

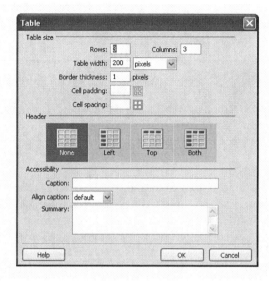

Figure 3-4: The Table dialog box.

Option	Description
Rows and **Columns**	Used to specify the number of rows and columns to be created in a table.
Table width	Used to specify the width of a table, either in pixels or as a percentage.
Border thickness	Used to place a visible border between table cells and around the table edges and to specify the thickness of the border. The larger the number, the thicker the border. If you do not want visible borders, enter zero in this text box.
Cell padding and **Cell spacing**	Used to control the distance between the edge of a cell and its content and the amount of space between table cells.
Header	Used to insert a header row for the table. The content in the header row is centered and appears bold. You can designate the top, left, or both portions of the table as the header row. If you do not want a header, select the **None** option.
Caption and **Align caption**	Used to insert and align a description that appears outside the table. You can align the caption to the center, top, bottom, left, or right. The default alignment is center.

Option	Description
Summary	Used to specify a summary of the table. You can use this option to enter a brief description about the contents of the table. This will be useful for users who need the aid of screen readers.

 If you specify the width of the table in pixels, the table width is fixed, even if the browser's window is resized. Percentage width is a dynamic measurement. It uses the width of the browser's window to determine the width of the table. Therefore, if a browser window is widened, the table will automatically widen.

Graphics in Table Cells

Just as you can select background colors for a table and a contrast cell color, you can also place images in the background of the table cells. Background images automatically get tiled within the cell irrespective of how tall or wide the cell becomes when the image is placed in it. You can specify the background image in the **Property Inspector.**

Nested Tables

Nested tables are tables placed within a cell. It allows you to create a complex design grid that will help in the alignment of text and graphics. You can use as many nesting levels as you need to create the grid you want.

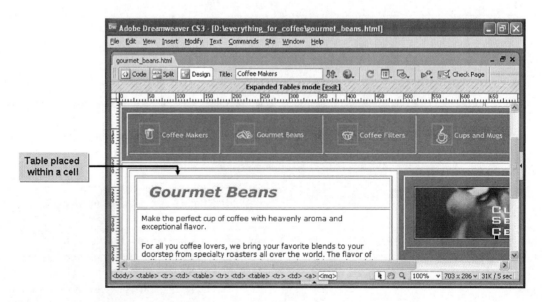

Figure 3-5: *Nested Table.*

Table Modes

You can create and manage tables using different modes. The following table describes the table modes.

Table Mode	Description
Standard mode	Tables are presented as a grid of rows and columns. This is the default mode in Dreamweaver CS3.
Layout mode	Allows you to draw tables and cells on the page. You can edit the basic table and cell properties to create the layout you want. You cannot insert tables while in this view.
Expanded mode	Temporarily adds extra cell spacing, padding, and borders to a table for easy editing. While creating nested tables, this option will clearly define where a table begins and where it ends, thereby allowing you to add text and images to individual cells easily.

How to Insert Tables

Procedure Reference: Create a Table Using the Standard Mode

To create a table using the **Standard** mode:

1. Place the insertion point at the desired location on the web page.
2. Display the **Table** dialog box.
   - On the **Insert** bar, on the **Common** tab, click the **Table** button.
   - Or, choose **Insert→Table.**
3. Specify the desired settings and click **OK.**
4. If necessary, on the **Insert** bar, select the **Layout** tab and click **Expanded** to work in the expanded mode.
5. Add content to the table.
   - Click in a cell and type the text or add an image.
   - Or, copy and paste the content using the **Paste Special** dialog box.
     a. Copy the desired content.
     b. Click in the desired cell.
     c. Choose **Edit→Paste Special.**
     d. In the **Paste Special** dialog box, select the desired option and click **OK.**
6. If necessary, select the desired region in the table and add a row or column.
   - Right-click the selected row or column, choose **Table,** and then choose the desired option to insert a row or column.
   - Choose **Insert→Table Objects** and choose the desired option.
   - Or, choose **Modify→Table** and choose the desired option.

When you are in the last cell of the table, you can press **Tab** to add a new row.

Table Selection Methods

You can select a particular cell, row, or a column in a table to apply formatting to it. There are a number of methods to select a region in a table.

● Place the mouse pointer on the left border of the desired row. When the mouse pointer changes to a right arrow, click to select the row.

● Place the mouse pointer on the top border of the desired column. When the mouse pointer changes to a down arrow, click to select the column.

● Click and drag to select multiple cells.

● Click in a cell, hold down **Shift,** and click in the cell up to which you want to select.

● Click in a cell to select it.

The Paste Special Dialog Box

The **Paste Special** dialog box allows you to determine the formatting options for the text pasted into Dreamweaver CS3.

It consists of four options:

● **Text only:** Allows you to paste unformatted text. All formatting in the original text, including line breaks and paragraphs, is removed.

● **Text with structure:** Allows you to retain the basic structure of the original text, but removes all formatting. You can retain options like paragraph structures, tables, and lists, but formatting such as bold and italics will not be retained.

● **Text with structure plus basic formatting:** Allows you to retain both structured and simple HTML formats from the original text.

● **Text with structure plus full formatting:** Allows you to retain all the structures, HTML formatting, and CSS styles from the original text.

Procedure Reference: Create a Table Using the Layout Mode

To create a table using the **Layout mode**:

1. Choose **View→Table Mode→Layout Mode.**
2. In the **Getting Started In Layout View** dialog box, click **OK.**
3. On the **Insert** bar, on the **Layout** tab, click the **Draw Layout Table** button.
4. Click at the desired location and drag to create a table.

You may not be able to create a table immediately below a text. Move the mouse pointer until it changes to a crosshair, and then click and drag to create the table.

5. Add a cell in the table.
   a. On the **Insert** bar, on the **Layout** tab, click the **Draw Layout Cell** button.
   b. Position the mouse pointer at the desired location and drag to create a table cell.

6. If necessary, in the **Property Inspector,** set the width and height of the cell.
   - Double-click in the **Width** text box and type a value.
   - Double-click in the **Height** text box and type a value.
7. Click in a cell and type the text or add an image to the table.

Procedure Reference: Format a Table

To format a table:

1. Select the desired region of the table.
2. Format the table using the **Property Inspector.**
   - In the **Property Inspector,** below the **Font** drop-down list, click the **Merges selected cells using spans** button to merge the selected cells.

 You can merge only the adjacent cells in the table. You can also merge the cells in an entire row or column.

   - Split a cell.
     a. In the **Property Inspector,** below the **Font** drop-down list, click the **Splits cell into rows or columns** button to split a selected cell.
     b. In the **Split Cell** dialog box, specify the options to split a cell into rows or columns and click **OK.**
   - Click in the **W** text box and type a value to change the width, and click in the **H** text box and type a value to change the height.
   - From the **Align** drop-down list, select the desired option to align the contents of the table.
   - Insert a background graphic into the table.
     a. In the **Property Inspector,** to the right of the **Bg** text box, click the **Background URL of cell** button.
     b. In the **Select Image Source** dialog box, navigate to the desired folder, select the file, and click **OK.**
   - Add a background color to the table.
     - Click in the second **Bg** text box and type the hexadecimal value of a color.
     - Or, to the left of the **Bg** text box, click the color swatch button and select the desired color.

Procedure Reference: Create a Nested Table

To create a nested table:

1. Click in a table cell.
2. On the **Insert** bar, on the **Common** tab, click the **Table** button.
3. Specify the settings in the **Table** dialog box and click **OK.**
4. Add content to the table.

ACTIVITY 3-2

Creating a Table

Data Files:

whatsnew.htm

Scenario:

You want to add information on the new flowers that have arrived in your gardens. You need to ensure consistent appearance of all elements on the web page.

What You Do	How You Do It
1. Create a table.	a. In the **Files** panel, double-click **whatsnew.htm.**
	b. Select the text **main text** and press **Delete.**
	c. On the **Insert** bar, select the **Common** tab and click the **Table** button.
	d. In the **Table** dialog box, double-click in the **Table width** text box and type **636**
	e. Click in the **Cell padding** text box and type **0**
	f. Click in the **Cell spacing** text box and type **0**

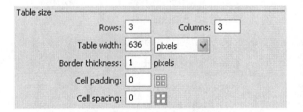

g. Click **OK** to create the table.

2. Add content to the table.

   a. In the second row, click in the first cell.

   b. On the **Common** tab, click the **Images** button and select **Image.**

   c. In the **Select Image Source** dialog box, select the **lily04.jpg** file and click **OK.**

   d. In the **Image Tag Accessibility Attributes** dialog box, in the **Alternate Text** text box, type *Pink Lily* and click **OK.**

   e. Insert the **lily05.jpg** image in the third column of the second row and set the alternate text to *White and Pink Lily*

   f. In the second row, click in the second cell.

   g. Type *Daylilies have just arrived! A wide variety of colors are available. Stop by and take a look, or check out our online listing.*

   h. Choose **File→Save.**

ACTIVITY 3-3
Formatting a Table

Data Files:

whatsnew.htm, whatsnewhead.gif

Scenario:
Some of the cells in the table appear to be large and the text and images are not aligned properly. In the first row, you want to add just one image, but there are some additional cells. Moreover, content in some of the cells is not clearly visible, which makes for difficult reading.

What You Do	How You Do It
1. Adjust the settings of the entire table.	a. Place the mouse pointer on the top border of the second column. When the mouse pointer changes to a down arrow, click to select the second column.

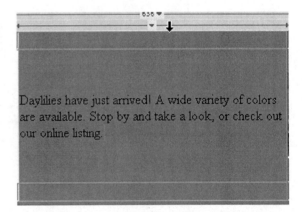

Daylilies have just arrived! A wide variety of colors are available. Stop by and take a look, or check out our online listing.

b. In the **Property Inspector,** click in the **W** text box, type *318* and press **Enter.**

c. Set the width of the left and right columns of the table to *159*

d. Click the border of the table to select it.

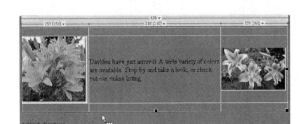

e. In the **Property Inspector,** click in the **Bg Color** text box, type *#FFFFFF* and press **Enter.**

f. Double-click in the **CellPad** text box, type *5* and press **Enter.**

g. Double-click in the **Border** text box, type *0* and press **Enter.**

---

2. Merge the cells in the first row to add an image.

a. Place the mouse pointer on the left border of the first row. When the mouse pointer changes to a right arrow, click to select the first row.

b. In the **Property Inspector,** below the **Font** drop-down list, click the **Merges selected cells using spans** button.

c. Click in the first row of the table.

d. In the **Files** panel, expand the **Graphics** folder.

e. Scroll down, click and drag the **whatsnewhead.gif** file to the first row of the table.

f. In the **Image Tag Accessibility Attributes** dialog box, in the **Alternate Text** text box, type *What's New* and click **OK.**

3. Align the content of the cells.

a. In the second row, second cell, click before the word **Daylilies.**

b. In the **Property Inspector,** from the **Vert** drop-down list, select **Top.**

c. In the second row, third cell, click to the left of the image.

d. In the **Property Inspector,** from the **Vert** drop-down list, select **Top.**

e. Save and close the file.

ACTIVITY 3-4

Creating a Table Using the Layout Mode

Data Files:

store.htm

Before You Begin:

In the **Files** panel, collapse the **Graphics** folder.

Scenario:

As you have not finalized the content to be displayed on the store information page, you are finding it difficult to set up a table to determine the layout. You want to add table cells as you create the web page.

What You Do	How You Do It
1. Display the page in the **Layout mode.**	a. In the **Files** panel, double-click **store.htm.**
	b. Choose **View→Table Mode→Layout Mode.**
	c. In the **Getting Started in Layout View** dialog box, click **OK.**

2. Create a table below the word **Directions.**

a. On the **Insert** bar, select the **Layout** tab and click the **Draw Layout Table** button.

b. Move the mouse pointer below the text **Directions** on the left side of the page, until the mouse pointer changes to a crosshair, and then click and drag to the bottom-right corner of the page to create a table.

c. In the **Property Inspector,** to the right of the **Fixed** option, double-click in the text box, type *636* and press **Enter.**

d. In the **Property Inspector,** double-click in the **Height** text box, type *194* and press **Enter.**

3. Add cells within the table.

a. If necessary, scroll down to view the entire table.

b. On the **Layout** tab, click the **Draw Layout Cell** button.

c. Click at the top-left corner of the table and drag to create a row 50 pixels in height that spans the width of the table.

d. Click the **Draw Layout Cell** button.

e. Click at the bottom-left corner of the first cell and drag to create a second row 50 pixels in height that spans the width of the table.

f. Click the **Draw Layout Cell** button.

g. Click at the bottom-left corner of the second cell and drag to add a third cell 200 pixels wide that spans the height of the table.

h. Select the cell that you just created and set the width to *159*

i. Add a fourth cell that is 400 pixels wide and spans the height of the table; set the width of the cell to *318* and add a fifth cell in the remaining space of the table.

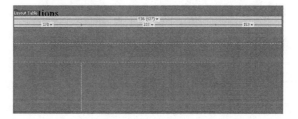

4. Add text into a table cell.

a. Scroll up and select the text above the table.

b. Choose **Edit→Cut** to cut the selected text.

c. Click in the middle column of the bottom row, and choose **Edit→Paste.**

d. Save and close the file.

OPTIONAL ACTIVITY 3-5
Working with Nested Tables

Data Files:

monthlypick.htm

Before You Begin:

Choose **View→Table Mode→Layout Mode** to exit the Layout mode.

Scenario:

You want to add information about the Iris flower, which has been picked as the flower of the month, in the monthlypick.htm file. You need to organize all the content in the iristext.htm file into the table in the monthlypick.htm file, but you need to ensure that the table does not look cluttered.

What You Do	How You Do It
1. Create a nested table.	a. In the **Files** panel, double-click **monthlypick.htm.**
	b. Click in the white cell.
	c. On the **Insert** bar, select the **Common** tab and click the **Table** button.
	d. In the **Table** dialog box, in the **Rows** text box, type **2**
	e. Double-click in the **Table width** text box and type **100**
	f. Click **OK** to create the table.

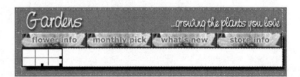

2. Place the text and images from the iristext.htm file into a table cell.

a. In the **Working** folder, open the **iristext.htm** file, copy all the text along with the images, and then close the file.

b. In the second row of the nested table, click in the second cell.

c. Choose **Edit→Paste Special.**

d. In the **Paste Special** dialog box, select the **Text with structure plus full formatting (bold, italic, styles)** option and click **OK.**

3. Reposition the graphic and link it to the correct image.

a. Click and drag the gray box to the cell immediately to the left.

b. Scroll down and click the gray box to select it.

c. In the **Property Inspector,** next to the **Src** text box, click the **Browse for File** button.

d. In the **Select Image Source** dialog box, select the **iris46.jpg** file and click **OK.**

e. Click to the left of the iris image.

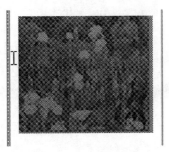

f. In the **Property Inspector,** from the **Vert** drop-down list, select **Top.**

g. Scroll up to view the image.

h. Save and close the file.

TOPIC C
Create Repeating Region Templates

You have created tables. Now, you may need to work on tables to display different amount of content based on your need. In this topic, you will create repeating region templates.

You have created a template that contains a table for entering the payroll information. But, you want the table size to vary depending on your requirement. Also, it would be easier if there is a method that allows you to expand the table just by the click of a button. Repeating regions in a template help you achieve this.

How to Create Repeating Region Templates

Procedure Reference: Create a Repeating Region Template

To create a repeating region template:

1. If necessary, create a new HTML template.
2. Select the region that needs to be defined as a repeating region.
3. On the **Insert** bar, on the **Common** tab, click the **Templates** button and choose **Repeating Region.**
4. In the **New Repeating Region** dialog box, in the **Name** text box, type a unique name and click **OK.**

 The name should be unique for each repeating region or editable region in a template.

5. Within the repeating region, select the region that needs to be defined as an editable region.
6. On the **Insert** bar, on the **Common** tab, click the **Templates** button and choose **Editable Region.**
7. In the **New Editable Region** dialog box, in the **Name** text box, type a unique name and click **OK.**
8. If necessary, create other editable regions.
9. Save and close the template.

Procedure Reference: Use a Repeating Region Template

To use a repeating region template:

1. Choose **File→New.**
2. In the **New Document** dialog box, select **Page from Template.**
3. Select the desired repeating region template and click **Create.**
4. In the repeating region header, click the Plus button (+) to add a row.
5. Add content to the editable region within the repeating region.
6. If necessary, add more content.
7. If necessary, click in a cell of the desired row and in the repeating region header, click the Minus button (–) to delete the row.

ACTIVITY 3-6

Creating a Repeating Region Template

Data Files:

pricing.dwt

Scenario:

You need to create a web page to display the pricing list of different flowers. As you may have to add more items to the list quite often, you want to automate the process of expanding the table.

What You Do	How You Do It
1. Create a repeating region template.	a. In the **Files** panel, expand the **Templates** folder.
	b. Double-click **pricing.dwt.**
	c. Place the mouse pointer on the left border of the last row. When the mouse pointer changes to a right arrow, click to select the last row.
	d. If necessary, on the **Insert** bar, select the **Common** tab.
	e. On the **Common** tab, click the **Templates** button and choose **Repeating Region.**

	f. In the **New Repeating Region** dialog box, in the **Name** text box, type *data* and click **OK.**

2. Add editable regions within the repeating region.

    a. In the last row, click in the first cell.

    b. On the **Insert** bar, on the **Common** tab, click the **Templates** button and choose **Editable Region.**

    c. In the **New Editable Region** dialog box, in the **Name** text box, type *product* and click **OK.**

    d. In the last row, insert an editable region in the second and third cells and name the regions as *picture* and *price* respectively.

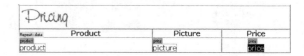

    e. Save and close the file.

3. Create a new document based on the **pricing** template.

    a. Choose **File→New.**

    b. In the **New Document** dialog box, verify that **Page from Template** is selected, and in the **Site** list box, verify that **Gardens** is selected.

    c. In the **Template for Site: "Gardens"** list box, select **pricing,** and click **Create.**

4. Enter content in the first row of the repeating region.

a. Double-click in the **product** cell, type *Yellow Daylily*

b. Double-click in the second cell and press **Delete.**

c. In the **Files** panel, expand the **Graphics** folder.

d. Click and drag the **lily02.jpg** file into the **picture** cell.

e. In the message box, check the **Don't show me this message again** check box and click **OK.**

f. In the **Image Tag Accessibility Attributes** dialog box, in the **Alternate Name** text box, type *Yellow Daylily* and click **OK.**

g. Double-click in the **price** cell and type *$13.45*

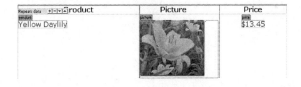

5. Complete the pricing list.

a. In the **Repeat: data** header, click the Plus button (**+**).

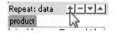

b. In the second row, in the **product** cell, type *Pink Daylily*

c. Double-click in the **picture** cell and press **Delete.**

d. Click and drag the **lily01.jpg** file into the **picture** cell.

e. In the **Image Tag Accessibility Attributes** dialog box, in the **Alternate Name** text box, type *Pink Daylily* and click **OK.**

f. Click in the **price** cell and type *$11.55*

g. In the **Repeat: data** header, click the Plus button (**+**).

h. In the third row, specify the following details:
- Product: *White Daylily*
- Picture: **lily03.jpg**
- Alternate text: *White Daylily*
- Price: *$12.95*

i. Save the file as ***price.htm*** in the **C:\084204Data\Adding Design Elements to Web Pages\Gardens** folder.

j. In the document window, click the **Close** button.

Lesson 3 Follow-up

In this lesson, you added design elements to web pages. This will result in the effective presentation of information and also enhance the visual appeal of a web page.

1. **When and why would you use the repeating region template?**

2. **What type of image would you use on your web pages? Why?**

4 | Working with Links

Lesson Time: 45 minutes

Lesson Objectives:

In this lesson, you will work with links.

You will:

- Create hyperlinks.
- Create email links.
- Create image maps.
- Create anchors.

Introduction

You created a number of web pages for your site. Now, you may want to make navigation between and within those pages easier. In this lesson, you will create links.

Assume that you are browsing a site and would like to get back to its home page. Without proper navigation controls, it would be difficult for you to move from one page to another. You can make your site more user-friendly and also ease the navigation by providing the necessary links at the appropriate locations.

TOPIC A
Create Hyperlinks

You added content to your web pages. Now, you may need to provide a navigation system that enables cross referencing of web page content. In this topic, you will create hyperlinks.

Browsing through a website to locate related information could become tedious when there are numerous web pages present. Providing hyperlinks to different web pages on the site will help the visitors to easily navigate to the desired page.

Hyperlinks

Definition:

Hyperlinks are links that reference another web page on the same website or a different website. By default, the text that contains a hyperlink is shown in blue and is underlined. When you click a hyperlink, the target web page, by default, opens in the same window. It can also be opened in a new window. Hyperlinks can be created on text or images.

Example:

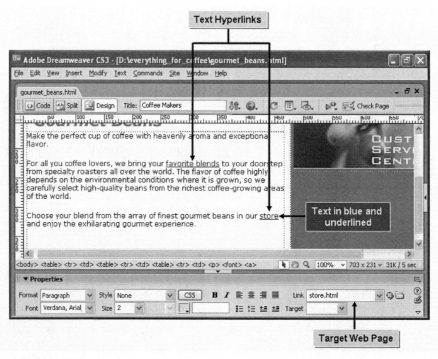

Figure 4-1: Hyperlinks on a web page.

Internal and External Hyperlinks

If the page you are linking to is stored in the same folder or directory as the current page, you just need to use the name of the file as the link. This link is known as internal hyperlink. When the links you create refer to files on another website, you need to specify the domain name along with the filename. This link is known as external hyperlink.

The <a> Tag

The <a> tag is used to create hypelinks for text and images. To refer to a text or an image on a different web page, you must specify the URL in the `href` attribute. The syntax to create an external hyperlink using the <a> tag is as follows:

<a href=URL**>**Text**</a>**

How to Create Hyperlinks

Procedure Reference: Create Hyperlinks

To create hyperlinks:

1. Select the desired text or image.

2. Create the hyperlink.

    *   In the **Property Inspector,** in the **Link** text box, click and type the file name or the URL to create the hyperlink.

     You must type the full URL for an external hyperlink. To avoid errors, you can copy the link from the browser and paste it in the **Link** text box.

    *   In the **Property Inspector,** to the right of the **Link** text box, click and drag the **Point to File** icon to the desired file in the **Files** panel.

    *   Create an internal hyperlink using the **Browse for File** button.

        a. In the **Property Inspector,** to the right of the **Link** text box, click the **Browse for File** button.

        b. In the **Select File** dialog box, navigate to the site folder, select the desired file and click **OK.**

    *   Or, create a hyperlink using the **Hyperlink** dialog box.

        a. On the **Common** tab, click the **Hyperlink** button.

        b. In the **Hyperlink** dialog box, create the hyperlink.

            *   In the **Link** text box, click and type the URL or the filename.

            *   To the right of the **Link** text box, click the **Browse** button, navigate to the site folder, select a file and click **OK.**

3. If necessary, in the **Property Inspector,** from the **Target** drop-down list, select **_blank** to open the link in a new browser window.

4. If necessary, verify the hyperlinks on a browser.

    a. Preview the web page in Internet Explorer.

    b. Click the hyperlink to view the target web page.

    c. Close the Internet Explorer window.

The Hyperlink dialog box

The **Hyperlink** dialog box allows you to create links to a web page. It contains several options.

The following table describes the options in the **Hyperlink** dialog box.

Option	Description
Text	Allows you to specify the text to which you want to create a link.
Link	Allows you to specify the web page to which you want to link to. You can also use the **Browse** button to browse to the file.
Target	Allows you to control how the links should open.
Title	Allows you to type a description of the page you are linking to. This description appears as a yellow pop-up box in the browser.
Access key	Allows you to specify a shortcut key to select the link.
Tab index	Allows you to specify the tab order.

Figure 4-2: *The Hyperlink dialog box.*

ACTIVITY 4-1

Creating Hyperlinks

Data Files:

whatsnew.htm, default.dwt, store.htm

Before You Begin:

1. If you are starting the course with the lesson "Working with Links", and the Gardens site was not previously defined in Dreamweaver, you must first define it by following the instructions in the activity "Defining a New Website", which is present in the lesson "Creating a Website", using the data from the C:\084204Data\Working with Links\Gardens folder.

2. If the Gardens site was previously defined in Dreamweaver, you must modify it by following the instructions in the activity "Changing the Local Root Folder of a Defined Website", which is present in the lesson "Creating a Website", so that it is based on the data from the C:\084204Data\Working with Links\Gardens folder.

3. In the **Files** panel, expand the **Site - Gardens** folder.

Scenario:

You have a page with information on the new flowers that have just arrived. You want to provide a reference to the price listing page on the flower information page so that visitors can check the price of the flower before placing their orders. Also, you want to update the template to provide access to the home page. You want to redirect visitors who would like to explore more information about the company to the **http://www.ourglobalcompany.com** website.

What You Do	How You Do It
1. Create an internal hyperlink.	a. In the **Files** panel, double-click **whatsnew.htm.**
	b. In the document window, in the last line, click before the word **online,** hold down **Shift,** and click after the word **listing** to select the text **online listing.**

c. In the **Property Inspector,** click in the **Link** text box, type *price.htm* and press **Enter** to create the internal hyperlink.

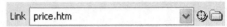

d. Choose **File→Save.**

---

2. Verify the internal hyperlink.

a. On the **Document** toolbar, click the **Preview/Debug in browser** button and choose **Preview in IExplore.**

b. Click the **online listing** link to view the **price.htm** page.

c. Close the Internet Explorer window.

d. In the document window, click the **Close** button to close the whatsnew.htm file.

---

3. Create an image link.

a. In the **Files** panel, expand the **Templates** folder and double-click **default.dwt.**

b. Select the **Gardens ...growing the plants you love** image.

c. In the **Property Inspector,** to the right of the **Link** text box, click the **Browse for File** button.

d. Navigate to the **C:\084204Data\Working with Links\Gardens** folder.

e. Select the **index.htm** file and click **OK** to create the image link.

f. Choose **File→Save.**

g. In the **Update Template Files** dialog box, click **Update** to update the links to all files.

h. In the **Update Pages** dialog box, click **Close.**

i. In the document window, click the **Close** button to close the **default.dwt** template.

---

4. Create an external hyperlink.

a. In the **Files** panel, double-click **store.htm.**

b. In the document window, scroll down, click at the bottom-right corner of the map and press **Enter.**

c. Type *More About Us*

Directions

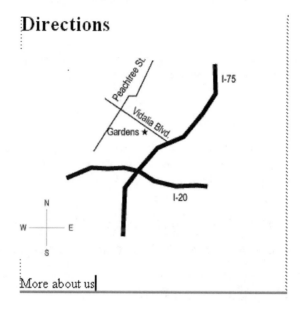

More about us

d. Hold down **Shift** and click before the word **More.**

e. In the **Property Inspector,** click in the **Link** text box, type **http:// www.ourglobalcompany.com** and press **Enter.**

f. From the **Target** drop-down list, select **_blank.**

g. Choose **File→Save** to save the file.

h. On the **Document** toolbar, click the **Preview/Debug in browser** button and choose **Preview in IExplore.**

i. Click the **More about us** link to view the **http://www.ourglobalcompany.com** website.

j. Close both the Internet Explorer windows.

TOPIC B

Create Email Links

You created hyperlinks. Now, you may want the site visitors to be able to send mail by accessing their email application directly from the web page. In this topic, you will create email links.

Visitors to your website will often look for ways to contact you through email. By providing email links, you can enable visitors to quickly send an email to request information or provide their suggestions and feedback on your site.

Email Link

The email link enables visitors to the site to quickly open their default email application from a web page. The address of the person who should be contacted with queries or feedback, is filled in automatically. Email links can be created on both text and images.

How to Create Email Links

Procedure Reference: Create an Email Link

To create an email link:

1. Select the desired text or image.
2. Create the email link.
   - In the **Property Inspector,** in the **Link** text box, click and type *mailto:* followed by the email address to be linked.

    Do not leave any space between the text **mailto** and the email address.

   - Or, create the email link using the **Email Link** dialog box.
     a. On the **Insert** bar, on the **Common** tab, click the **Email Link** button.
     b. If necessary, in the **Email Link** dialog box, in the **Text** text box, type the desired text.
     c. In the **E-Mail** text box, type the email address and click **OK.**
3. If necessary, verify the email link on a browser.
   a. Preview the web page in Internet Explorer.
   b. Click the email link to open the email application with the email address of the contact person filled in automatically.
   c. Close the email application and the Internet Explorer window.

ACTIVITY 4-2

Create E-mail Link

Data Files:

store.htm

Scenario:

You want the site visitors to be able to post their queries or send feedback about the website to the site administrator.

What You Do	How You Do It
1. Create an email link.	a. In the document window, scroll up, click after the number **(717) 555-1444,** and press **Enter.**
	b. Type *Email:* and press **Spacebar.**

Gardens

715 Vidalia Boulevard
Atlanta, GA 30018

(717) 555-1444

Email:

c. On the **Common** tab, click the **Email Link** button, ⬚ to open the **Email Link** dialog box.

d. In the **Text** text box, type *info@ourglobalcompany.com*

e. In the **E-Mail** text box, click and type
    info@ourglobalcompany.com

f. Click **OK** to create the email hyperlink.

g. Choose **File→Save** to save the file.

2. Verify the email link.

a. On the **Document** toolbar, click the **Preview/Debug in browser** button and select **Preview in IExplore.**

b. Click the **info@ourglobalcompany.com** email link to open the email application.

c. In the **New Message** window, in the **To** text box, observe that the email address is filled in automatically.

d. Close the **New Message** window.

e. Close the Internet Explorer window.

f. Close the file.

3. **True or False? Email links can be created only for text.**

    ___ True

    ___ False

TOPIC C
Create Image Maps

You have created links on images. You can also link a section of an image to a web page. In this topic, you will create image maps.

You have listed the products and services of your company on the home page. Instead of providing text hyperlinks for all the pages on the site, you can represent the links graphically in a single image and turn selected regions of the image to act as links.

The Hotspot

A *hotspot* is an area on an image, which can be clicked to open a linked web page. Hotspots can take rectangular, oval, or a polygon shape. You can create a hotspot using the hotspot tools in the **Property Inspector.**

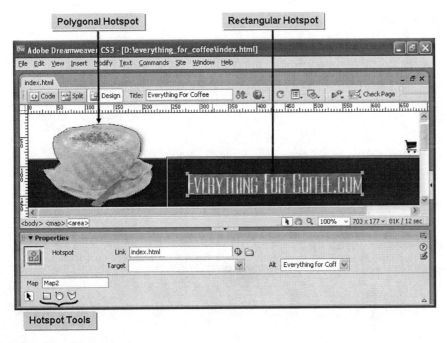

Figure 4-3: Image with hotspots.

The Image Map

An *image map* is a single image that contains one or more hotspots. These hotspots can be used to link different regions of the image to different web pages rather than splitting the image to link to different pages.

How to Create Image Maps

Procedure Reference: Create an Image Map

To create an image map:

1. Select an image.
2. In the **Property Inspector,** in the **Map** section, select the desired hotspot tool.
3. Place the mouse pointer at the desired location, and drag to create a hotspot.
4. In the **Adobe Dreamweaver CS3** message box, click **OK.**
5. In the **Property Inspector,** in the **Alt** text box, type an alternate name for the image.
6. Link the hotspot to the desired web page using the **Property Inspector.**
7. If necessary, create other hotspots and link them to the pages.
8. If necessary, resize the hotspot section.
    a. In the **Property Inspector,** click the **Pointer Hotspot** button.
    b. On the image, click the desired hotspot section, and drag its handle to move or resize the selected hotspot section.
9. If necessary, verify the hotspot links on a browser.
    a. Preview the web page in Internet Explorer.
    b. Click the hotspots on the image map to view the respective pages.
    c. Close the Internet Explorer window.

ACTIVITY 4-3
Creating Image Maps

Data Files:

index.htm

Scenario:

The home page on your website contains an image that lists the different sections on the website. You want the user to be able to access the section of the website they are interested in by simply clicking the section name on the image on a home page.

What You Do	How You Do It
1. Create rectangular hotspots in the image.	a. In the **Files** panel, double-click the **index.htm** file.
	b. In the document window, select the image at the center of the page.
	c. In the **Property Inspector,** in the **Map** section, click the **Rectangular Hotspot Tool** button.

d. Click in the upper-left corner of the image and drag it to the bottom-right corner of the **Flower Info** section to create a rectangle over the **Flower Info** section of the image.

e. In the **Adobe Dreamweaver CS3** message box, click **OK.**

f. In the **Property Inspector,** click in the **Alt** text box, type *Flower Information* and press **Enter** to set the alternate text of the image.

g. In the **Property Inspector,** double-click in the **Link** text box, type ***flowerinfomain.htm*** and press **Enter** to link the hotspot.

h. Similarly, create hotspots for the other parts of the image; set the alternate text to **Monthly Pick, What's New,** and **Store Info;** link them with the **monthlypick.htm, whatsnew.htm,** and **store.htm** files, respectively.

2. Resize the **Flower Information** hotspot section.

a. In the **Property Inspector,** in the **Map** section, click the **Pointer Hotspot** button.

b. In the document window, scroll up and select the **Flower Info** hotspot section.

c. In the **Flower Info** hotspot, click at the lower-right corner of the border and drag it diagonally upwards until the hotspot section surrounds the text **Flower Info** in the image.

d. Position the hotspot such that the text **Flower Info** is centered within it.

e. Choose **File→Save** to save the file

f. On the **Document** toolbar, click the **Preview/Debug in browser** button and choose **Preview in IExplore.**

g. Click the **Flower Info** section of the image to view the **flowerinfomain.htm** page.

h. Click the **Back** button.

i. Click the **Monthly Pick** section of the image to view the **monthlypick.htm** page.

j. Close the Internet Explorer window.

k. Close the file.

TOPIC D
Create Anchors

You know to create links to different web pages. In the course of your work, you may need to create links to a particular section within a web page. In this topic, you will create anchors.

Assume that you have an exhaustive amount of information on your web page. When a user needs to find a particular information on the page, he may have to go through the entire content to locate it. By providing links at the appropriate location, you can enable users to navigate directly to the information they are interested in.

The Anchor

An *anchor* is a link that takes visitors to a particular location on a page. You can create a named anchor for each section and provide links to them at suitable locations on the web page. This will help the user to quickly return to a section without having to scroll through the page.

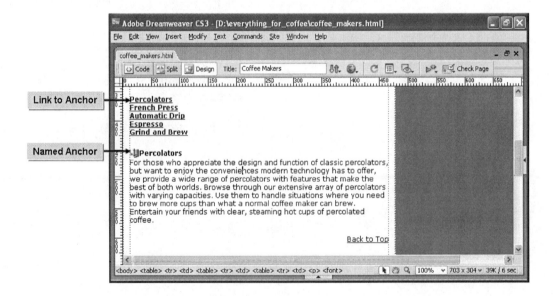

Figure 4-4: A web page with an anchor and links to the anchor.

How to Create Anchors

Procedure Reference: Create Anchor Links

To create anchor links:

1. In the document window, place the insertion point before the text for which you want to create an anchor.

2. Open the **Named Anchor** dialog box.

    *   On the **Common** tab, click the **Named Anchor** button.

    *   Or, choose **Insert→Named Anchor.**

3. In the **Anchor name** text box, type a name and click **OK** to create an anchor.

4. Select the text to which you want to link the anchor.

5. Create a link to the named anchor.

    *   In the **Property Inspector,** in the **Link** text box, click and type **#** followed by the anchor name to create a link to the named anchor.

    *   In the **Property Inspector,** to the right of the **Link** text box, click the **Point to File** button and drag it to the anchor marker on the web page.

    *   Or, create a link using the **Hyperlink** dialog box.

        ■   In the **Link** text box, click and type **#** followed by the anchor name.

        ■   Or, from the **Link** drop-down list, select the desired anchor.

 You can also link to a named anchor on another page, by typing the file name followed by the # sign and the named anchor.

6. If necessary, verify the anchor links on a browser.

    a. Preview the web page in Internet Explorer.

    b. Click an anchor link to move to a particular section on the web page.

    c. Close the Internet Explorer window.

ACTIVITY 4-4
Creating Anchor Links

Data Files:

annuals.htm

Scenario:

You have information on different types of flowers on your annuals.htm page. You do not want your visitors to scroll down the long page to view information about the flower they are interested in. Instead, you want to provide quick navigation to each section of the page.

What You Do	How You Do It
1. Create anchors on the **annuals.htm** page.	a. In the **Files** panel, double-click **annuals.htm.**
	b. Click before the **Pansies** heading.
	c. On the **Common** tab, click the **Named Anchor** button.
	d. In the **Named Anchor** dialog box, in the **Anchor name** text box, type *pansies* and click **OK.**
	e. In the document window, observe that an anchor marker appears before the **Pansies** heading, indicating that a named anchor has been created.
	 Annuals Pansies | Petunias | Sunflowers | Zinnias **Pansies**
	f. Create anchors called *petunias*, *sunflowers*, and *zinnias* for the flower headings, respectively.
2. Create links for the different anchors.	a. In the document window, scroll up to view the **Pansies** heading.

b. Double-click the word **Pansies** above the **Pansies** heading.

c. In the **Property Inspector,** in the **Link** text box, click and type *#pansies* and press **Enter.**

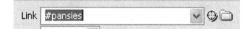

d. Create anchor links for the text **Petunias, Sunflowers,** and **Zinnias** to the named anchors **petunias, sunflowers,** and **zinnias.**

e. Choose **File→Save** to save the file.

f. On the **Document** toolbar, click the **Preview/Debug in browser** button and choose **Preview in IExplore.**

g. Click the **Sunflowers** link to move to the **Sunflowers** section.

h. Scroll up to view the anchor links.

i. Click the **Zinnias** link to move to the **Zinnias** section.

j. Close the Internet Explorer window.

k. Close the file.

Lesson 4 Follow-up

In this lesson, you created text links and image links. You also created image maps and anchors. Links aid visitors in navigating through a site and accessing web pages quickly.

1. **When would you create image links for your website? Why?**

2. **Which links would you necessarily have on all web pages? Why?**

5 | Working with Frames

Lesson Time: 45 minutes

Lesson Objectives:

In this lesson, you will work with frames.

You will:

- Create framesets.
- Enhance frames in a frameset.

Introduction

You have created links on your web pages to enhance the navigability of your website. So far you have worked with web pages that are displayed one at a time in the browser window. However, at times you may need to display more than one web page in the same browser window. In this lesson, you will work with frames.

When you design a website, you may want the name and links to different parts of the website to be uniform on all pages. It is tedious to recreate these elements on all web pages. A better option would be to use frames.

TOPIC A
Create Framesets

In this lesson, you are going to work with frames. To work with frames, you first need a frameset that contains multiple frames. In this topic, you will create a frameset.

As a web designer your aim is to design web pages that are easy to navigate and present required information in an organized way. To achieve this goal, you may need to select the appropriate layout mechanism for the web pages you design. Creating framesets would help you to lay out web pages in such a way that they are easy to navigate and present well-organized information.

Frames

Frames provide a way to lay out a web page by dividing the browser window into multiple regions. Each frame is independent and can display a web page that is different from those displayed in the rest of the browser window. Most websites display logos, advertisements, the title of the website in a frame at the top, a set of navigation links in a narrow frame on the left, and the main content in the large frame that occupies the rest of the page.

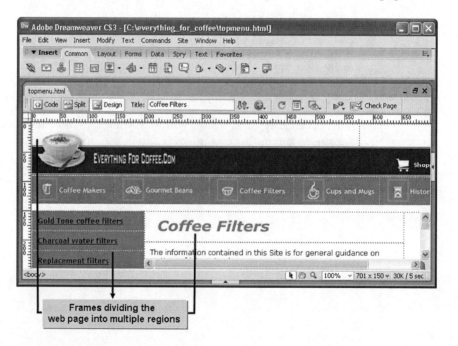

Figure 5-1: A web page displaying frames.

Disadvantages of Frames

The use of frames does have its own set of potential problems. For example, if a viewer links to a page directly that should be displayed within a frameset, there may not be navigation links available to get to other parts of the site. In addition, it is more difficult to print or bookmark a page within a frameset.

Framesets

A *frameset* stores information about the layout and properties of the frames used on a web page. The information includes the number of frames, their size, placement, and the web page that is displayed initially in each frame. This information would be used by the browser to lay out the web page.

The Frames Panel

The **Frames** panel provides a visual representation of the arrangement of frames on a web page. Each frame in the **Frames** panel is identified by its name and is surrounded by a border. Groups of frames are surrounded by thick borders. You can select a single frame, multiple frames, or the entire frameset by clicking the appropriate border.

How to Create Framesets

Procedure Reference: Create a Frameset

To create a frameset:

1. Choose **File→New.**
2. In the **New Document** dialog box, select the **Page from Sample** category.
3. In the **Sample Folder** list box, select **Frameset.**
4. In the **Sample Page** list box, select the required frameset.
5. Click **Create** to create the frameset.
6. In the **Frame Tag Accessibility Attributes** dialog box, enter a title for each frame.
    a. From the **Frame** drop-down list, select a frame.
    b. In the **Title** text box, double-click and type a title for the frame.
    c. Click **OK.**
7. If necessary, resize the frames as required.
8. If necessary, on the Document toolbar, in the **Title** text box, modify the title of the web page.
9. Enter a name for each frame in the frameset.
    a. Choose **Window→Frames.**
    b. In the **Frames** panel, select a frame.
    c. In the **Property Inspector,** in the **Frame** name text box, double-click and type a frame name.
10. Choose **File→Save Frameset As.**
11. If necessary, in the **Save As** dialog box, navigate to the required folder.
12. In the **File name** text box, type a file name for the frameset.
13. Click **Save** to save the frameset.

Procedure Reference: Populating the Frames in a Frameset

To populate the frames in a frameset:

1. Open the frameset file that you created.
2. Add content to the frames in the frameset.
    *   Load an existing web page in a frame.

    a.   In the **Frames** panel, select the required frame.

    b.   In the **Property Inspector,** using the **Src** property, load an existing web page.

- To the right of the **Src** text box, click the **Browse for File** button, and in the **Select HTML File** dialog box, select the required file.

- To the right of the **Src** text box, drag the **Point to File** button to the required file in the **Files** panel.

- Or, click in the **Src** text box and type the path to the required file.

- Create a web page in a frame.

    a.   In the document window, click in a frame.

    b.   Add text, images, and other required elements in the frame.

    c.   If necessary, choose **Modify→Page Properties** and in the **Page Properties** dialog box, modify the page properties.

    d.   Choose **File→Save Frame As** and save the frame with an appropriate name.

3.   Choose **File→Save All** to save the changes.

Procedure Reference: Link Frames

To link frames:

1.   Select the desired text or image in a frame.

2.   Link the selected text or image to the desired page.

3.   In the **Property Inspector,** from the **Target** drop-down list, select the desired option to set the target for the link page.

4.   Choose **File→Save All** to save the frame links.

Options in the Target Drop-Down List

The Target drop-down list provides four options. The following table describes the options.

Option	*Description*
_blank	Creates a new browser window and displays the linked web page in it.
_self	Loads the linked web page into the current frame. It is the default value.
_top	Targets the entire browser window. Removes all existing framesets and loads the linked page in the current window.
_parent	Targets the entire browser window. Removes only the frameset that directly contains the current frame.

ACTIVITY 5-1
Creating a Frameset

Data Files:

flowertop.htm, flowerinfomain.htm

Before You Begin:

1. If you are starting the course with the lesson "Working with Frames", and the Gardens site was not previously defined in Dreamweaver, you must first define it by following the instructions in the activity "Defining a New Website", which is present in the lesson "Creating a Website", using the data from the C:\084204Data\Working with Frames\ Gardens folder.

2. If the Gardens site was previously defined in Dreamweaver, you must modify it so that it is based on the new data from the C:\084204Data\Working with Frames\Gardens folder. Follow the instructions in the activity "Changing the Local Root Folder of a Defined Website", which is present in the lesson "Creating a Website".

Scenario:

You have linked the web pages on your website. As you navigate through them, you realize that it would be helpful if the content in certain regions remain the same across all the pages, while the content in a few other regions change per the visitors' requests.

What You Do	How You Do It
1. Create a web page with frames.	a. Choose **File→New**.
	b. In the **New Document** dialog box, select the **Page from Sample** category.
	c. In the **Sample Folder** list box, select **Frameset.**
	d. In the **Sample Page** list box, select **Fixed Top, Nested Left** and click **Create** to create the frameset.

2.	Modify the accessibility attributes of the leftFrame and resize it.	a.	In the **Frame Tag Accessibility Attributes** dialog box, from the **Frame** drop-down list, select **leftFrame.**
		b.	Double-click in the **Title** text box and type *flowernav*
		c.	Click **OK.**
		d.	In the document window, place the mouse pointer on the border line between leftFrame and mainFrame until it shows a double-headed arrow, and drag it to the 150-inch mark on the horizontal ruler to make leftFrame larger.
3.	Modify the title and the attributes of the frameset page.	a.	On the Document toolbar, in the **Title** text box, click before the word **Untitled,** hold down **Shift** and click after the word **Document.**
		b.	Type *Flower Information - Gardens*
		c.	Choose **Window→Frames.**
		d.	In the **Frames** panel, select **leftFrame.**
		e.	In the **Property Inspector,** double-click in the **Frame name** text box, type *navbar* and press **Enter.**
		f.	Choose **File→Save Frameset As.**
		g.	In the **Save As** dialog box, navigate to the **C:\084204Data\Working with Frames\ Gardens** folder.
		h.	In the **File name** text box, type *flowerinfo.htm* and click **Save** to save the frameset.
4.	Insert web pages in the **topFrame** and **mainFrame.**	a.	In the **Frames** panel, select **topFrame.**
		b.	In the **Property Inspector,** to the right of the **Src** text box, click the **Browse for File** button.
		c.	In the **Select HTML File** dialog box, select the **flowertop.htm** page and click **OK.**
		d.	Observe that the **flowertop.htm** page appears in the topFrame of the frameset.
		e.	Link the mainFrame to the **flowerinfomain.htm** page.

5. Create a web page in the **navbar** frame.

a. In the document window, click in the **navbar** frame.

b. Choose **File→Save Frame As.**

c. In the **File name** text box, type *flowernav.htm* and click **Save** to save the frameset.

d. In the document window, in the **navbar** frame, insert the **annuals.gif** image located within the **Graphics** folder, and set the alternate text to *Annuals*

e. Click to the right of the annuals image and press **Enter** to start a new paragraph.

f. In the document window, in the navbar frame, insert the **perennials.gif** image located within the **Graphics** folder and set the alternate text to *Perennials*

g. Choose **Modify→Page Properties.**

h. In the **Page Properties** dialog box, click in the **Background Color** text box, type *#669900* and click **OK.**

i. Choose **File→Save All** to save all the frames and the frameset.

TOPIC B
Enhance Frames

You have created framesets and added content to frames. Now, you may need to make the content in the frames noticeable. In this topic, you will enhance frames.

When you design web pages using frames, you have to organize the content in such a way that the screen is not cluttered with too much information and that the user is able to find the necessary details easily. This will improve the appearance of the frames and attract visitors to the website.

Frame Properties

Frame properties allow you to enhance the appearance of the frames on a web page. These properties can be set using the **Property Inspector.** The following table describes the properties.

Property	Description
Scroll	Specifies whether the frame displays scroll bars or not.
No resize	Disables the visitor's ability to resize a frame.
Borders	Specifies whether the frame displays a border or not.
Border color	Allows you to specify a color for the frame's border.
Margin width	Specifies the amount of space in pixels for the left and right margins of the frame.
Margin height	Specifies the amount of space in pixels for the top and bottom margins of the frame.

How to Enhance Frames

Procedure Reference: Set Frameset Properties

To set frameset properties:

1. In the **Frames** panel, click the border of the frameset to select it.

2. In the **Property Inspector,** in the **RowCol Selection** section, select the required row or column of the frameset.

3. Specify the size of the selected row or column.

    ● In the **Row** section, in the **Value** text box, type a number and press **Enter.**

    ● In the **Column** section, in the **Value** text box, type a number and press **Enter.**

4. From the **Units** drop-down list, select the required unit.

5. If necessary, in the **Border width** text box, double-click and type a number to specify the size of the border.

6. If necessary, from the **Borders** drop-down list, select the required option.

7. If necessary, in the **Border color** text box, type a color value for the border.

8. Choose **File→Save Frameset** to save the properties of the frameset.

Procedure Reference: Set Frame Properties

To set frame properties:

1. In the **Frames** panel, select the required frame.

2. In the **Property Inspector,** modify the selected frame's properties.

    ● Double-click in the **Frame name** text box and type a name for the frame.

    ● From the **Scroll** drop-down list, select the desired scrolling option.

    ● In the **Margin width** text box, enter a value to set the margin width of the frame.

    ● In the **Margin height** text box, enter a value to set the margin height of the frame.

    ● Check the **No resize** check box to disable viewers from resizing the frame in their browser windows.

    ● From the **Borders** drop-down list, select the required option.

    ● In the **Border color** text box, type a color value for the border.

3. Choose **File→Save All** to save the changes.

ACTIVITY 5-2

Enhancing Frames

Data Files:

flowerinfo.htm

Scenario:

You have created a web page with multiple frames. However, you find that certain portions of a frame on the web page are hidden from view. Also, you want to improve navigation among the different web pages and fine tune the organization of content in the frames.

What You Do	How You Do It
1. Resize **topFrame** and the **navbar** frame.	a. In the document window, click the lower border of the **topFrame** and drag it down until the text **Flower Information** is covered.

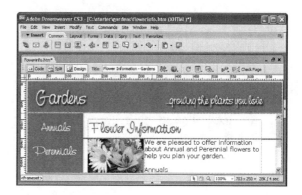

b. In the **Frames** panel, click the border surrounding **navbar** and **mainFrame** to select both the frames.

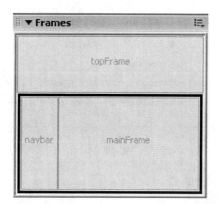

c. In the **Property Inspector,** in the **RowCol Selection** section, verify that the left tab is selected.

d. In the **Column** section, double-click in the **Value** text box, type *159* and press **Enter.**

2.	Set the frame properties for mainFrame.	a.	In the **Frames** panel, select **mainFrame**.
		b.	In the **Property Inspector,** click in the **Margin width** text box, type *5* and press **Enter.**
		c.	Click in the **Margin height** text box, type *5* and press **Enter.**
		d.	From the **Scroll** drop-down list, select **Auto.**
3.	Link the images in the **navbar** frame and **topFrame** to the appropriate web pages.	a.	In the **navbar** frame, select the **Annuals** image.
		b.	In the **Property Inspector,** click in the **Link** text box, type *annuals.htm* and press **Enter.**
		c.	In the **Property Inspector,** from the **Target** drop-down list, select **mainFrame.**
		d.	In the **navbar** frame, link the perennials image to the **perennials.htm** web page, and set the target to **mainFrame.**
		e.	In **topFrame,** link the **Gardens** logo to the **index.htm** page.
		f.	In the **Property Inspector,** from the **Target** drop-down list, select **_top.**
4.	Preview the files on the browser.	a.	Choose **File→Save All** to save all the frames and the frameset.
		b.	Choose **File→Preview in Browser→ IExplore** to preview the frameset in Internet Explorer.
		c.	In the **navbar** frame, click the **Annuals** image.
		d.	Observe that the annuals.htm file is loaded into **mainFrame.**
		e.	In the **topFrame,** click the garden's logo.
		f.	Observe that the index.htm file is loaded in the browser window.
		g.	Close the browser window.
		h.	Choose **File→Close** to close the flowertop.htm file.

Lesson 5 Follow-up

In this lesson you worked with frames. This enables you to create multiple regions within a single web page and to display independent content in them.

1. **While choosing a layout mechanism for your web page, in what situations will you opt for frames?**

2. **Which frame properties do you use frequently to enhance the frames on your web pages? Why?**

6 | Uploading a Website

Lesson Time: 1 hour(s), 10 minutes

Lesson Objectives:

In this lesson, you will upload a website.

You will:

- Ensure accessibility standards for a website.
- Upload files onto a site.

Introduction

You have organized the content of your website and interconnected the web pages that constitute the website. Now, you may want the other users to access the website. In this lesson, you will upload a website.

People with different abilities and varied systems would access the information on your website. You need to ensure that the information on the web pages is conveyed to all as intended. By validating content and uploading it, you can achieve this.

TOPIC A
Ensure Accessibility

You have created all the required web pages for your website and you are ready to upload the files onto a site. However, before uploading, you need to check the functionality of the web pages so that visitors of the website do not encounter any problems. In this topic, you will validate the web pages and ensure their accessibility.

Your website will reach a wider audience when many users access it. Checking the website for accessibility standards will help you ensure that the website is accessible to everyone.

Accessibility Standards

Web accessibility refers to the process of enabling people with visual, motor, auditory, and other disabilities to access web pages. To ensure web accessibility, web developers need to check that the web pages they develop adhere to accessibility standards. Significant accessibility standards are Section 508 of the Federal Rehabilitation Act and the World Wide Web Consortium Web Accessibility Initiative.

Section 508 Standards

Section 508 of the Federal Rehabilitation Act states that federal agencies should ensure that employees as well as people with disabilities are able to access technology. Section 508 standards are as follows:

- §1194.22 Web-based intranet and Internet information and applications:

   a.   A text equivalent for every non-text element shall be provided (e.g., using "alt" or "longdesc" in element content).

   b.   Equivalent alternatives for any multimedia presentation shall be synchronized with the presentation.

   c.   Web pages shall be designed so that all information conveyed with color is also available without color, for example from context or markup.

   d.   Documents shall be organized so that they are readable, without requiring an associated style sheet.

   e.   Redundant text links shall be provided for each active region of a server-side image map.

   f.   Client-side image maps shall be provided instead of server-side image maps, except where the regions cannot be defined with an available geometric shape.

   g.   Row and column headers shall be identified for data tables.

   h.   Markup shall be used to associate data cells and header cells for data tables that have two or more logical levels of row or column headers.

   i.   Frames shall be titled with text that facilitates frame identification and navigation.

   j.   Pages shall be designed to avoid causing the screen to flicker with a frequency greater than 2 Hz and lower than 55 Hz.

   k.   A text-only page, with equivalent information or functionality, shall be provided to make a website comply with the provisions of this part, when compliance cannot be accomplished in any other way. The content of the text-only page shall be updated whenever the primary page changes.

   l.   When pages utilize scripting languages to display content or to create interface elements, the information provided by the script shall be identified with functional text that can be read by assistive technology.

   m.   When a web page requires that an applet, plug-in, or other application be present on the client system to interpret page content, the page must provide a link to a plug-in or applet that complies with §1194.21(a) through (l).

   n.   When electronic forms are designed to be completed online, the form shall allow people using assistive technology to access the information, field elements, and functionality required for completion and submission of the form, including all directions and cues.

   o.   A method that permits users to skip repetitive navigation links shall be provided.

   p.   When a timed response is required, the user shall be alerted and given sufficient time to indicate that more time is required.

The Board interprets paragraphs (a) through (k) of this section as consistent with the following priority 1 Checkpoints of the Web Content Accessibility Guidelines 1.0 (WCAG 1.0) (May 5, 1999) published by the Web Accessibility Initiative of the World Wide Web Consortium.

Section 1194.22 Paragraph	WCAG 1.0 Checkpoint
(a)	1.1
(b)	1.4
(c)	2.1
(d)	6.1
(e)	1.2
(f)	9.1
(g)	5.1
(h)	5.2
(i)	12.1
(j)	7.1
(k)	11.4

Paragraphs (l), (m), (n), (o), and (p) of this section are different from WCAG 1.0. Web pages that conform to WCAG 1.0, level A (i.e., all priority 1 checkpoints) must also meet the requirements of paragraphs (l), (m), (n), (o), and (p) of this section to comply with this section. WCAG 1.0 is available at **www.w3.org/TR/1999/WAI-WEBCONTENT-19990505**.

Supporting International Languages

The attribute lang = language-code [CI] specifies the base language of text content and also an element's attribute values. The default value of this particular attribute is not known. A user agent may use the language information that is specified using the lang attribute, to control rendering in many different ways.

W3C Standards (HTML Validation)

There are some important validation methods that should be followed to ensure that users do not encounter any problems while accessing a website. You must use an automated accessibility tool and browser validation tool, and validate syntax and style sheets. You need to use a text-only browser or emulator and multiple graphic browsers, with sounds and graphics loaded, graphics not loaded, sounds not loaded, no mouse, frames, scripts, style sheets, and applets not loaded to validate a page. In addition, you can use several browsers, old and new, and also self-voicing browsers, screen readers, magnification software, or a small display, to perform the validation. You must also use spelling and grammar checkers and must review the document for clarity and simplicity. Alternatively, you can request that people with disabilities review the documents.

W3C Deprecated Tags

When new constructs are being used, certain elements or attributes become outdated. These are called deprecated elements or attributes. The reference manual of W3C defines deprecated elements in appropriate locations and also clearly marks them as deprecated. For backward compatibility, user agents should continue to support deprecated elements. For example, <applet>, <basefont>, <center>, <dir>, <font>, <isindex>, <menu>, <s>, <strike>, and <u> are deprecated tags in the HTML 4.01 specification.

WCAG Priority 1 Checklist

The Web Accessibility Initiative of the World Wide Web Consortium has developed access guidelines that are included in Section 508, and a website should contain elements, such as Alt text or verbal tags, to make it easier for the user to access the web pages. For example, people with sight disabilities can rely on screen readers, which translate the onscreen objects into audible output, and also on Braille displays. The elements of the WCAG Priority 1 checklist are as follows:

- Provide a text equivalent for every non-text element (for example, "alt", "longdesc" or using a linked document). This includes: images, graphical representations of text (including symbols), image map regions, animations (e.g., animated GIFs), applets and programmatic objects, ASCII art, frames, scripts, images used as list bullets, spacers, graphical buttons, sounds (played with or without user interaction), standalone audio files, audio tracks of video, and video.

- Ensure that all information conveyed with color is also available without color, for example from context or markup.

- Clearly identify changes in the natural language of a document's text and any text equivalents (for example, captions).

- Organize documents so they may be read without style sheets. For example, when an HTML document is rendered without associated style sheets, it must still be possible to read the document.

- Ensure that equivalents for dynamic content are updated when the dynamic content changes.

- Until user agents allow users to control flickering, avoid causing the screen to flicker.

- Use the clearest and simplest language appropriate for a site's content.

- Provide redundant text links for each active region of a server-side image map.

- Provide client-side image maps instead of server-side image maps, except where the regions cannot be defined with an available geometric shape.

- For data tables, identify row and column headers.

- For data tables that have two or more logical levels of row or column headers, use markup to associate data cells and header cells.

- Title each frame to facilitate frame identification and navigation.

- Ensure that pages are usable when scripts, applets, or other programmatic objects are turned off or not supported. If this is not possible, provide equivalent information on an alternative accessible page.

- Until user agents can automatically read aloud the text equivalent of a visual track, provide an auditory description of the important information of the visual track of a multimedia presentation.

- For any time-based multimedia presentation (for example, a movie or animation), synchronize equivalent alternatives (for example, captions or auditory descriptions of the visual track) with the presentation.

- If, after best efforts, you cannot create an accessible page, provide a link to an alternative page that uses W3C technologies, is accessible, has equivalent information (or functionality), and is updated as often as the inaccessible (original) page.

> The alternate text in images is used by software that reads web pages aloud. If there is no alternate text, then the software reads the file name. Specifying alternate text for every image on your site will help ensure compliance with Section 508 for accessibility.

WCAG Priority 2 Checklist

The elements of the WCAG Priority 2 checklist are as follows:

- Ensure that foreground and background color combinations provide sufficient contrast when viewed by someone with color defects or when viewed on a black and white screen. (Priority 2 for images, Priority 3 for text.)

- When an appropriate markup language exists, use markup rather than images to convey information.

- Create documents that validate to published formal grammar.

- Use style sheets to control layout and presentation.

- Use relative rather than absolute units in markup language attribute values and style sheet property values.

- Use header elements to convey document structure and use them according to specification.

- Mark up lists and list items properly.

- Mark up quotations. Do not use quotation markup for formatting effects such as indentation.

- Ensure that dynamic content is accessible or provide an alternative presentation or page.

- Until user agents allow users to control blinking, avoid causing content to blink (that is, change the presentation at a regular rate, such as turning on and off).

- Until user agents provide the ability to stop the refresh, do not create periodically auto-refreshing pages.

- Until user agents provide the ability to stop auto-redirect, do not use markup to redirect pages automatically. Instead, configure the server to perform redirects.

- Until user agents allow users to turn off spawned windows, do not cause pop-ups or other windows to appear and do not change the current window without informing the user.

- Use W3C technologies when they are available and appropriate for a task, and use the latest versions when supported.

- Avoid deprecated features of W3C technologies.

- Divide large blocks of information into more manageable groups where natural and appropriate.

- Clearly identify the target of each link.

- Provide metadata to add semantic information to pages and sites.

- Provide information about the general layout of a site (for example, a site map or table of contents).

- Use navigation mechanisms in a consistent manner.

- Do not use tables for layouts unless the table makes sense when linearized. Otherwise, if the table does not make sense, provide an alternative equivalent (which may be a linearized version).

- If a table is used for layouts, do not use any structural markup for the purpose of visual formatting.

- Describe the purpose of frames and how frames relate to each other if it is not obvious by frame titles alone.

- Until user agents support explicit associations between labels and form controls, for all form controls with implicitly associated labels, ensure that the label is properly positioned.

- Associate labels explicitly with their controls.

- For scripts and applets, ensure that event handlers are input device-independent.

- Until user agents allow users to freeze moving content, avoid movement in pages.

- Make programmatic elements such as scripts and applets directly accessible or compatible with assistive technologies. (Priority 1 if functionality is important and not presented elsewhere, otherwise Priority 2.)

- Ensure that any element that has its own interface can be operated in a device-independent manner.

- For scripts, specify logical event handlers rather than device-dependent event handlers.

The Results Panel

The **Results** panel contains tools that you can use to search for information on a website and validate the website for accessibility and browser compatibility issues. These tools are grouped in different tabs based on their functionality. The following table describes the tabs.

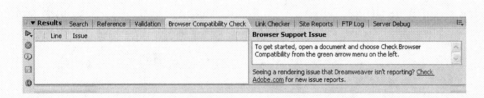

Figure 6-1: *The Results panel and its various tools.*

Tab	Description
Search	Allows you to find and replace text on web pages.
Reference	Provides reference information about the different languages and elements you might use.
Validation	Allows you to check the code on a web page. Dreamweaver can validate web pages in many languages.

Tab	Description
Browser Compatibility Check	Checks the browser compatibility of the various elements used on a web page.
Link Checker	Lists external links, broken links, and orphaned files that you may want to identify and delete.
Site Reports	Allows you to generate **Workflow** and **HTML Reports.**
FTP Log	Allows you to view all FTP file transfer activities.
Server Debug	Provides information on how to debug a ColdFusion application.

 Files that are created but not referenced on the website are referred to as orphaned files.

Adobe CSS Advisor

Adobe CSS Advisor is a website that provides information, suggestions and tips on the latest browser, and code issues in Dreamweaver. If a browser compatibility issue is found on the web pages you have developed, a link is provided on the **Browser Compatibility Check** tab of the **Results** panel. Accessing this link will enable you to read the documentation about the issue on the **Adobe CSS Advisor** website. In addition to referring information on the **Adobe CSS Advisor** website, you can post your comments and suggestions. You can also add new issues.

Validator Preferences

The Dreamweaver validator checks the code on web pages for errors. Using the *validator preferences*, you can specify the languages that you want to check the code against. You can also specify the exact problems that need to be checked and the messages that are to be displayed.

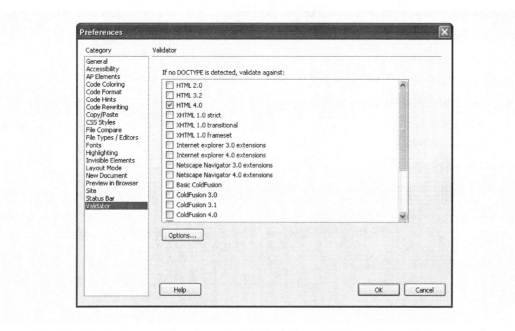

Figure 6-2: The Preferences dialog box displaying the validator preferences.

Site Reports

The **Reports** dialog box allows you to generate two types of reports for a site, namely, **Workflow** and **HTML Reports. Workflow** reports help to improve collaboration among the team members. **HTML Reports** validate a website for accessibility, missing alternate text, untitled documents, and other attributes that help to optimize code. The site reports are displayed on the **Site Reports** tab of the **Results** panel.

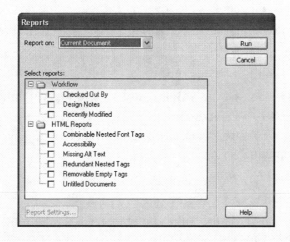

Figure 6-3: The Reports dialog box.

How to Ensure Accessibility

Procedure Reference: Set Validator Preferences

To set validator preferences:

1. Open the **Preferences** dialog box.

   - Choose **Edit→Preferences.**

   - Or, in the **Results** panel, select the **Validation** tab, click the **Validate** button and choose **Settings.**

2. In the **Preferences** dialog box, in the **Category** list box, select **Validator.**

3. In the **Validator** section, specify the desired options.

 You can choose only one version of each language to validate against.

4. If necessary, change the Validator options.

   a. In the **Validator** section, click **Options.**

   b. In the **Validator Options** dialog box, in the **Display** section, uncheck the options you do not need.

   c. In the **Check For** section, uncheck the options you do not need.

   d. Click **OK** to save the changes to the validator options.

5. In the **Preferences** dialog box, click **OK** to save the preferences.

Procedure Reference: Validate Web Pages

To validate web pages:

1. In the **Files** panel, double-click a file to open it.

2. Choose **Window→Results,** and in the **Results** panel, select the **Validation** tab.

3. Validate the current document.

   - Choose **File→Validate→Markup.**

   - In the **Results** panel, on the **Validation** tab, click the **Validate** button and choose **Validate Current Document.**

   - On the Document toolbar, click the **Validate markup** button and choose **Validate Current Document.**

   - Or, press **Shift+F6.**

4. If necessary, validate the entire site.

   - In the **Results** panel, on the **Validation** tab, click the **Validate** button and choose **Validate Entire Current Local Site.**

   - Or, on the Document toolbar, click the **Validate markup** button and choose **Validate Entire Current Local Site.**

5. If necessary, hold down **Ctrl** and select multiple files to validate.

   - In the **Results** panel, on the **Validation** tab, click the **Validate** button and choose **Validate Selected Files in Site.**
   - Or, on the Document toolbar, click the **Validate markup** button and choose **Validate Selected Files in Site.**

6. On the **Validation** tab, in the **File** column, identify the files that contain errors and in the **Description** column, read through the error description.

7. If necessary, correct errors on the relevant web pages.

8. If necessary, on the **Validation** tab, click **Save Report** and save the report.

9. If necessary, browse the report in a browser window.

   a. On the **Validation** tab, click **Browse Report** to view the report in the browser window.

   b. In the **File** column, click a file link to view the file.

   c. Click the **Close** button to close the browser window.

10. Choose **File→Save** to save the file.

Procedure Reference: Check Target Browsers

To check target browsers:

1. In the **Files** panel, double-click a file to open it.

2. Choose **Window→Results** to display the **Results** panel.

3. Select the **Browser Compatibility Check** tab.

4. If necessary, change the target browser settings.

   a. Click the **Check Browser Compatibility** button and choose **Settings.**

   b. In the **Target Browsers** dialog box, in the **Minimum browser versions** section, check the check boxes of the required browsers and from the drop-down list next to each selected browser, select the required version.

   c. Click **OK** to save the settings.

5. Check the target browser for the current document.

   - Choose **File→Check Page→Browser Compatibility.**
   - In the **Results** panel, on the **Browser Compatibility Check** tab, click the **Check Browser Compatibility** button and choose **Check Browser Compatibility.**

6. On the **Browser Compatibility Check** tab, identify the issues listed.

7. If necessary, correct the browser compatibility issues on the web page.

8. If necessary, on the **Browser Compatibility Check** tab, click the **Save Report** button and save the report.

9. If necessary, on the **Browser Compatibility Check** tab, click the **Browse Report** button to view the report in the browser window.

10. Choose **File→Save** to save the file.

Procedure Reference: Generate Site Reports

To generate site reports:

1. In the **Files** panel, double-click a file to open it.

2. If necessary, hold down **Ctrl** and select multiple files.

3. Choose **Window→Results** to display the **Results** panel, and then select the **Site Reports** tab.

4. Open the **Reports** dialog box.

   - On the **Site Reports** tab, click the **Reports** button.

   - Or, in the **Files** panel group, from the **Options** menu, choose **Site→Reports.**

5. In the **Reports** dialog box, in the **Select reports** section, check the necessary options.

   - Below the **Workflow Reports** sub-tree, check the necessary options.

   - Below the **HTML Reports** sub-tree, check the necessary options.

6. In the **Reports dialog box,** from the **Report on** drop-down list, select an option.

7. If necessary, disable the report settings for the **Accessibility** option.

   a. In the **Select reports** section, below the **HTML Reports** sub-tree, check the **Accessibility** check box and click **Report Settings.**

   b. In the **Accessibility** dialog box, in the **Category - Rule** column, select an option.

   c. If necessary, expand the option and select a sub-category.

   d. Click **Disable** to disable the selected accessibility standard.

   e. Click **OK** to save the changes.

8. Click **Run.**

9. In the **Results** panel, on the **Site Reports** tab, in the **File** column, identify the files that contain errors and in the **Description** column, read through the error description.

10. If necessary, correct the errors on the web pages.

11. If necessary, on the **Site Reports** tab, click **Save Report** and save the report.

12. Choose **File→Save** to save the file.

ACTIVITY 6-1

Ensuring Accessibility Standards

Data Files:

flowertop.htm, store.htm, index.htm

Before You Begin:

1. If you are starting the course with the lesson "Uploading a Website", and the Gardens site was not previously defined in Dreamweaver, you must first define it by following the instructions in the activity "Defining a New Website", which is present in the lesson "Creating a Website", using the data from the C:\084204Data\Uploading a Website\ Gardens folder.

2. If the Gardens site was previously defined in Dreamweaver, you must modify it so that it is based on the new data from the C:\084204Data\Uploading a Website\Gardens folder. Follow the instructions in the activity "Changing the Local Root Folder of a Defined Website", which is present in the lesson "Creating a Website".

Scenario:

You have developed all the pages required for your website. But, before you allow others to access it, you need to ensure that all the pages on the site function as intended and people with different abilities and different systems are able to access it.

What You Do	How You Do It
1. Check whether the web pages adhere to HTML standards.	a. In the **Files** panel, expand the **Site - Gardens** folder.
	b. Double-click the **flowertop.htm** file to open it.
	c. Choose **Window→Results** to display the **Results** panel.
	d. In the **Results** panel, select the **Validation** tab.
	e. Click the **Validate** button, [▶] and choose **Validate Current Document**.
	f. On the **Validation** tab, observe that an error has been listed and in the **Description** column, observe the error description.

2.	Rectify the error in the flowertop.htm file.	a.	In the **Property Inspector,** click **Page Properties** to display the **Page Properties** dialog box.
		b.	In the **Category** section, verify that **Appearance** is selected.
		c.	In the **Appearance** section, in the **Background color** text box, click and type *#669900*
		d.	Click **OK** to apply the correct value for the background color.
		e.	Choose **File→Save All** to save the changes.
		f.	On the **Validation** tab, click the **Validate** button and choose **Validate Current Document.**
		g.	In the **Description** column, observe the message that no errors or warnings have been found.

flowertop.htm   No errors or warnings found.[HTML 4.0]

		h.	Choose **File→Close** to close the flowertop.htm file.
3.	Select the target browser to check the Gardens local site.	a.	In the **Results** panel, select the **Browser Compatibility Check** tab.
		b.	Click the **Check Browser Compatibility** button and choose **Settings.**
		c.	In the **Target Browsers** dialog box, in the **Internet Explorer** drop-down list, verify that **6.0** is selected.
		d.	Uncheck the **Firefox, Internet Explorer for Macintosh, Netscape, Opera** and **Safari** check boxes.
		e.	Click **OK** to set Microsoft Internet Explorer 6.0 as the target browser.

4. Check the home page for target browser compatibility.

    a. In the **Files** panel, double-click the **index.htm** file to open it.

    b. In the **Results** panel, on the **Browser Compatibility Check** tab, click the **Check Browser Compatibility** button and choose **Check Browser Compatibility.**

    c. On the **Browser Compatibility Check** tab, observe that no error messages are displayed.

    d. Choose **File→Close** to close the file.

5. Generate site reports of web pages that have missing alternate text and are untitled.

    a. In the **Results** panel, select the **Site Reports** tab.

    b. Click the **Reports** button.

    c. In the **Reports** dialog box, from the **Report on** drop-down list, select **Entire Current Local Site.**

    d. In the **Select reports** section, under the **HTML Reports** sub-tree, check the **Missing Alt Text** and **Untitled Documents** check boxes.

    e. Click **Run** to generate the site report.

6. Check the site reports and make the necessary changes.

a. On the **Site Reports** tab, in the **Description** coulmn, observe the warning message that the store.htm file uses the default title **Untitled Document.**

b. If necessary, in the **Files** panel, scroll down to view the store.htm file.

c. Double-click **store.htm.**

d. In the document window, in the **Title** text box, click before the word **Untitled,** hold down **Shift** and click after the word **Document.**

e. Type *Store Info* and press **Enter.**

f. Choose **File→Save** to save the store.htm file.

g. In the **Results** panel, on the **Site Reports** tab, in the **Description** coulmn, observe the warning message that the store.htm file has a **Missing "alt" attribute.**

h. If necessary, in the document window, scroll down to view the content below the title **Store Information.**

i. In the document window, below the title **Store Information,** in the first column on the left, select the image.

j. In the **Property Inspector,** click in the **Alt** text box, and type *Flower Field* and press **Enter.**

k. Choose **File→Save** to save the store.htm file.

7. Check the accessibility standards of the site.

a. In the **Results** panel, on the **Site Reports** tab, click the **Reports** button to display the **Reports** dialog box.

b. In the **Select reports** section, below the **HTML Reports** sub-tree, check the **Accessiblity** check box.

c. Click **Report Settings.**

d. In the **Accessibility** dialog box, select **W3C/WCAG P.2 accessibility.**

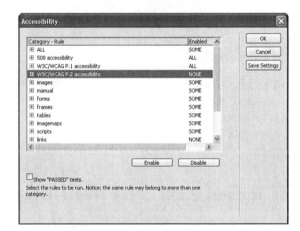

e. Click **Disable** to disable the **W3C/WCAG P.2 accessibility** standard.

f. Click **OK** to save the report settings.

g. In the **Reports** dialog box, click **Run** to generate the site report.

8. Save the report.

a. In the **Results** panel, on the **Site Reports** tab, click the **Save Report** button.

b. In the **Save As** dialog box, navigate to the **C:\084204Data\Uploading a Website\ Gardens** folder.

c. In the **File name** text box, click and type *myreport* and click **Save.**

d. Choose **File→Close All** to close all the files.

TOPIC B
Upload Files onto a Site

You have validated the web pages on your website and ensured that they adhere to accessibility standards. The next step would be to upload the files to a remote location so that others can access them. In this topic, you will upload files onto a site.

In an educational institution, a library serves as a central repository for books that students can access. Similarly, a central repository for your website can be a common folder that anyone can access. By uploading the site files to the common folder you can ensure that your web pages are accessible to everyone.

Site Maps

A *site map* is a hierarchical visual representation of the structure of a website. It displays the home page as the starting point and shows the pages of the website two levels deep. It helps you to identify the structure of the website and examine the links between the pages. On the site map, broken links are displayed in red. You can save the site map in the BMP or PNG format.

The Get and Put Methods

The Get and Put methods allow you to transfer files between a local site and a remote site. The *Get method* allows you to copy files from a remote site to a local site. The *Put method* allows you to upload files from a local site onto a remote site. If any errors are encountered during upload or download, Dreamweaver logs them for your review. The Get and Put methods can be accessed by using the **Get File(s)** and **Put File(s)** buttons on the **Files** panel.

Internet Service Providers

After you have built your site, you will want it to be available to other users. To do that, you will have to transfer them to a web server. If you work with a university, a government agency, or a large company or an organization, you often have a dedicated Internet connection and a web server. If you are an individual or work for a small company, you can use a web hosting service, which provides space on a web server for your use. Additionally, if you have an account with an online service provider, or ISP, often that account comes with a certain amount of web space. Most web hosting services enable you to use your own domain name (that is, www.[yourcompany].com), whereas ISPs generally do not offer this option. If you publish your site to your ISP, generally the address follows the format www.[ispname].com/[username].

Site Upload

If you have an account with an ISP or a web-hosting service, or if you have access to your own web server, you can upload the site to that remote server. In order to successfully transfer the files to the server you are using, you need several main pieces of information such as account information and the FTP address to access the server. An ISP or a web-hosting service will issue a user name and password associated with your account, and will give you the File Transfer Protocol (FTP) address.

How to Upload Files Onto a Site

Procedure Reference: Examine the Site Map

To examine the site map:

1. In the **Files** panel, click the **Expand to show local and remote sites** button.
2. Click the **Site Map** button and choose the desired option.
3. If necessary, expand the links in the site map.
4. If necessary, specify the home page of the site.

    a. Choose **View→Site Map Options→Layout.**

    b. In the **Site Map Layout** section, in the **Home page** text box, type the path of the site home page and click **OK.**

5. If necessary, view the page titles.

    -   Choose **View→Site Map Options→Show Page Titles.**

    -   Or, press **Ctrl+Shift+T.**

6. If necessary, choose **View→Site Map Options→Show Dependent Files** to view the list of images and other dependent files that are used on the page.

7. Click the **Collapse to show only local or remote site** button to collapse the **Files** panel.

Procedure Reference: Check the Links on the Site

To check the links on the site:

1. In the **Files** panel, double-click a file to open it.
2. Choose **Windows→Results** to display the **Results** panel, and in the **Results** panel, select the **Link Checker** tab.
3. From the **Show** drop-down list, select an option to view broken links, external links, or orphaned files.
4. Check the links for the current document.

    -   Choose **File→Check Page→Links.**

    -   In the **Results** panel, on the **Link Checker** tab, click the **Check Links** button and choose **Check Links in Current Document.**

    -   Or, press **Shift+F8.**

5. If necessary, check the links for the entire site.

    -   In the **Results** panel, on the **Link Checker** tab, click the **Check Links** button and choose **Check Links For Entire Current Local Site.**

    -   In the **Files** panel, right-click the site root folder and choose **Check Links→Entire Local Site.**

    -   In the **Files** panel group, from the **Options** menu, choose **Site→Check Links Sitewide.**

    -   Choose **Site→Check Links Sitewide.**

    -   Or, press **Ctrl+F8.**

6. If necessary, select the required files on the site and check the links.

    a. In the **Files** panel, hold down **Ctrl** and select the required files.

    b. Check the links for the selected files.

- In the **Results** panel, on the **Link Checker** tab, click the **Check Links** button and choose **Check Links For Selected Files in Site.**

- Or, in the **Files** panel, right-click the selected files and choose **Check Links→ Selected Files.**

7. If necessary, on the **Link Checker** tab, select a link and correct it.

8. If necessary, on the **Link Checker** tab, click the **Save Report** button and save the report.

9. Choose **File→Save** to save the file.

Procedure Reference: Upload a Site

To upload a site:

1. Open the **Manage Sites** dialog box.

   - In the **Files** panel group, from the **Options** menu, choose **Site→Manage Sites.**

   - In the **Files** panel, from the **Site** drop-down list, select **Manage Sites.**

   - Or, choose **Site→Manage Sites.**

2. Select the desired site and click **Edit.**

3. In the **Site Definition** dialog box, select the **Advanced** tab and in the Category section, select **Remote Info.**

4. In the **Remote Info** section, select an access method to access the files from a remote server and configure it.

   - Select FTP as the access method and apply the required settings for configuring it.

     a. From the **Access** drop-down list, select **FTP.**

     b. In the **FTP host** text box, enter the ISP or web hosting service's FTP address.

     c. If necessary, in the **Host Directory** text box, enter the sub-directory path to place the site files inside a sub-directory within the remote site's root folder.

     d. In the **Login** and **Password** text boxes, enter the login and password assigned by the ISP or web-hosting service.

   - Select Local/Network as the access method and apply the required settings for configuring it.

     a. From the **Access** drop-down list, select **Local/Network.**

     b. To the right of the **Remote folder** text box, click the folder icon.

     c. In the **Choose remote root folder for site** dialog box, navigate to the required folder.

     d. If necessary, create a new folder.

     e. Open the required remote folder and click **Select.**

5. In the **Site Definition** dialog box, click **OK.**

6. In the **Manage Sites** dialog box, click **Done.**

7. If necessary, delete the working folder of the site.

   a. In the **Files** panel, select the working folder and press **Delete.**

   b. In the **Adobe Dreamweaver CS3** dialog box, click **Yes** to confirm the deletion of the folder.

8. In the **Files** panel, select the root folder of the site.

9. In the **Files** panel, click the **Put File(s)** button to upload the site files.

10. In the **Adobe Dreamweaver CS3** dialog box, click **OK** to upload the entire site to the remote server.

11. In the site map, examine the files on the remote site.

   a. In the **Files** panel, click the **Expand to show local and remote sites** button.

   b. Click the **Site Map** button and choose the desired option.

   c. In the left pane, observe that the files on the remote site are displayed.

12. Click the **Collapse to show only local or remote site** button.

Procedure Reference: Update Site Files

To update site files:

1. Update the required files on the local site.

2. If necessary, change the links on the site.

   a. In the **Files** panel group, from the **Options** menu, choose **Site→Change Link Sitewide.**

   b. In the **Change Link Sitewide** dialog box, next to the **Change all links to** text box, click the folder icon.

   c. If necessary, in the **Select Link to Change** dialog box, navigate to the required folder.

   d. Select the desired file and click **OK.**

   e. In the **Change Link Sitewide** dialog box, next to the **Into links to** text box, click the folder icon.

   f. If necessary, in the **Select New Link** dialog box, navigate to the required folder.

   g. Select the desired file and click **OK.**

   h. In the **Change Link Sitewide** dialog box, click **OK.**

3. In the **Update Files** dialog box, click **Update** to update all the links to the renamed file.

4. In the **Files** panel group, from the **Options** menu, choose **Edit→Select Newer Local** to select the changed files.

5. In the **Files** panel, click the **Put File(s)** button.

6. Click **Yes** to upload the dependent files along with the changed files.

ACTIVITY 6-2

Uploading a Site

Data Files:

flowerinfomain.htm, navbar.htm

Scenario:

You have completed the entire website and tested it thoroughly. For others to view the web pages, you need to place them in a location that every user can access.

What You Do	How You Do It
1. Examine the site map.	a. In the **Files** panel, click the **Expand to show local and remote sites** button.
	b. Click the **Site Map** button and choose **Map and Files** to view the site map in the left pane and the site files in the right pane.
	c. In the left pane, expand **store.htm** and then expand **index.htm.**
	d. Observe how the web pages are linked.
	e. Collapse **store.htm.**
	f. Choose **View→Site Map Options→Show Dependent Files** to view the list of images and other dependent files that are used on the page.
	g. In the left pane, scroll to the right of the window to view the remaining dependent files.
	h. Click the **Collapse to show only local or remote site** button to collapse the **Files** panel.

2. Perform the site link check.

   a. In the **Files** panel group, from the **Options** menu, choose **Site→Check Links Sitewide.**

   b. In the **Results** panel, on the **Link Checker** tab, in the **File** column, double-click **/flowerinfomain.htm.**

   c. In the **Property Inspector,** double-click in the **Link** text box, type *store.htm* and press **Enter.**

   d. Choose **File→Save** to save the flowerinfomain.htm file.

   e. On the **Link Checker** tab, from the **Show** drop-down list, select **External Links** to view the external links.

   f. On the **Link Checker** tab, from the **Show** drop-down list, select **Orphaned Files** to view the files that do not have any links to them.

   g. In the **Orphaned Files** column, select **/navbar.htm** and press **Delete.**

   h. In the **Adobe Dreamweaver** dialog box, click **Yes** to delete the file.

   i. In the **Results** panel group, from the **Options** menu, choose **Close panel group** to close the **Results** panel group.

   j. Choose **File→Close** to close the flowerinfomain.htm file.

3. Edit the site information of the Gardens site.

   a. Choose **Site→Manage Sites.**

   b. In the **Manage Sites** dialog box, click **Edit.**

   c. In the **Site Definition for Gardens** dialog box, select the **Advanced** tab.

   d. In the **Category** list box, select **Remote Info.**

   e. From the **Access** drop-down list, select **Local/Network.**

4. Specify the local test site folder.	a. To the right of the **Remote Folder** text box click the folder icon.
	b. In the **Choose remote root folder for site Gardens** dialog box, navigate to the **C:\084204Data\Uploading a Website** folder.
	c. Click the **Create New Folder** button.
	d. In the **New Folder** text box, type *Test Gardens* and press **Enter** two times.
	e. Click **Select** to select the Test Gardens folder as the remote folder.
	f. In the **Site Definition for Gardens** dialog box, click **OK.**
	g. In the **Adobe Dreamweaver CS3** dialog box, click **OK.**
	h. In the **Manage Sites** dialog box, click **Done.**
5. Upload the site files.	a. In the **Files** panel, select the working folder and press **Delete.**
	b. In the **Adobe Dreamweaver CS3** dialog box, click **Yes** to confirm the deletion of the folder.
	c. In the **Files** panel, select the **Site - Gardens** folder.
	d. In the **Files** panel, click the **Put File(s)** button.
	e. In the **Adobe Dreamweaver CS3** dialog box, click **OK** to upload the entire site.
	f. In the **Files** panel, click the **Expand to show local and remote sites** button.
	g. Click the **Site Files** button.
	h. In the left pane, observe that the files on the remote site are displayed.
	i. Click the **Collapse to show only local or remote site** button.

ACTIVITY 6-3
Uploading Changed Files

Data Files:

price.htm

Scenario:

You have checked all the files on the site by running the site on a local server. The Flower Info link in the monthlypick.htm file is incorrectly sourced to the flowerinfomain.htm file. You have uploaded the site with this incorrect link. In addition to this correction, you also need to update the price of the pink daylily flower in the price.htm file and modify the site files on the server as well, without affecting the links to other pages that are dependent on them.

What You Do	How You Do It
1. Update the price of the pink Daylily flower.	a. In the **Files** panel, double-click the **price.htm** file to open it.
	b. In the second row, in the **Price** column, select **$11.55**.
	c. Type **$12.00**
	d. Choose **File→Save** to save the changes.
	e. Choose **File→Close** to close the price.htm file.
2. Preview the **Monthly Pick** page of the site.	a. In the **Files** panel, double-click the **monthlypick.htm** file to open it.
	b. Choose **File→Preview in Browser→ IExplore.**
	c. In Internet Explorer, click the **Flower Info** link.
	d. Observe that the link navigates to the flowerinfomain.htm file instead of the flowerinfo.htm file.
	e. Close the Internet Explorer window.
	f. Choose **File→Close** to close the monthlypick.htm file.

3. Change the links to the **Flower Info** page.

   a. In the **Files** panel group, from the **Options** menu, choose **Site→Change Link Sitewide.**

   b. In the **Change Link Sitewide (Site - Gardens)** dialog box, next to the **Change all links to** text box, click the folder icon.

   c. In the **Select Link to Change** dialog box, navigate to the **C:\084204Data\Uploading a Website\Gardens** folder.

   d. Select **flowerinfomain.htm** and click **OK.**

   e. In the **Change Link Sitewide (Site - Gardens)** dialog box, next to the **Into links to** text box, click the folder icon.

   f. In the **Select New Link** dialog box, select **flowerinfo.htm** and click **OK.**

   g. In the **Change Link Sitewide (Site - Gardens)** dialog box, click **OK.**

   h. In the **Update Files** dialog box, click **Update** to update the links.

4. Upload the changed files to the remote server.

   a. In the **Files** panel, select the **Site - Gardens** folder.

   b. In the **Files** panel group, from the **Options** menu, choose **Edit→Select Newer Local** to select the changed files.

   c. In the **Files** panel, click the **Put File(s) button** to upload the changed files.

   d. In the **Dependent Files** dialog box, **click Yes** to have Dreamweaver upload the dependent files along with the changed files.

Lesson 6 Follow-up

In this lesson, you validated your web pages and uploaded them onto a site. This ensures that your website is available on a remote location and users can access it.

1. **Why is it a good idea to examine the site map before uploading the website?**

2. **Why do you need to check the links on your web pages before uploading them?**

Follow-up

In this course, you designed, built, and uploaded a website using the features in the Dreamweaver application. You will now be able to create websites that look appealing and easily navigable.

1. **How would you customize the Dreamweaver environment to suit your work requirements?**

2. **When would you use tables to present information on a web page?**

3. **Why do you need a site map?**

What's Next?

Adobe® Dreamweaver® CS3: Level 2 is the next course in this series. In this course, you will use the advanced features of Dreamweaver to create professional looking web pages.

A | Adobe Certified Expert (ACE) Program®

Adobe® Dreamweaver® CS3 (Level 1) ACE Exam Objectives

The Adobe Certified Expert (ACE) Program is for graphic designers, web designers, developers, systems integrators, value-added resellers, and business professionals, who seek recognition for their expertise with specific Adobe products. Certification candidates must pass a product proficiency exam in order to become an Adobe Certified Expert.

Selected Element K courseware addresses Adobe Certified Expert certification skills. The following tables indicate where Adobe Dreamweaver CS3 skills are covered in the Adobe Dreamweaver CS3: Level 1 course. For example, 3–A indicates the lesson and topic number applicable to that skill.

Objective	*Adobe Dreamweaver CS3: Level 1*
1.0 Understanding Web technologies	
1.1 Given an HTML tag, explain the purpose of that tag (tags include: div, span, table, a).	3–B, 4–A
1.2 Describe the difference between CSS classes and IDs.	
1.3 Explain how JavaScript is used on the client in Web pages.	
1.4 List and describe the features and functionality of ftp and how it is used in Dreamweaver.	
2.0 Planning sites	
2.1 Define a local site by using the Manage Sites dialog box.	2–A
2.2 Manage site definitions for local, remote, and testing server information.	2–A
2.3 Describe considerations related to case-sensitive links.	2–A
2.4 Given a scenario, define the structure of a site.	2–D, 6–B

Objective	Adobe Dreamweaver CS3: Level 1
2.5 Given a scenario, select and set the appropriate resolution for a site.	2–B
2.6 List and describe considerations related to designing a site for multiple platforms and browsers.	6–A
2.7 List and describe the features Dreamwever provides for Accessibility Standards/Section 508 compliance.	6–A
2.8 Explain how templates are used to architect for reuse and consistency.	2–E
2.9 Create pages by using CSS starter pages.	
2.10 Explain how to extend Dreamweaver by using Extensions.	2–B
2.11 Given a scenario, set development Preferences.	1–C
2.12 Given a scenario, choose the proper method to layout a page (methods include: tables, layers, CSS Box model).	3–B
2.13 Incorporate graphics and rich media onto a website.	3–A
3.0 Designing pages	
3.1 List and describe how to navigate the Dreamweaver UI.	1–C
3.2 Use Find and Replace including support for regular expressions.	
3.3 Create and use page templates.	2–E
3.4 Create and maintain Cascading Style Sheets (CSS).	
3.5 Create and use reusable page objects by using library items.	
3.6 Explain the purpose of and how to use Server-side includes.	
3.7 Create and use code Snippets.	
3.8 Given a method, layout a page (methods include: Table Layout, Layers, Expanded Tables mode).	3–B
3.9 List and describe the options for creating and saving new pages.	2–B
3.10 Set document properties by using the Document Properties dialog box.	2–C
3.11 Layout a page by using guides.	1–B
3.12 List and describe the options available for formatting the structure of a document (options include: paragraph breaks, line breaks, non-breaking spaces, tables).	2–C

Objective	Adobe Dreamweaver CS3: Level 1
3.13 List and describe, and resolve issues related to browser compatibility.	6–A
3.14 Use JavaScript behaviors to implement page functionality (behaviors include: Pop- Up Menus, Open Browser Window, Swap Image, Go To URL).	
3.15 Add Flash elements to a Web page (options include: text, buttons, video, paper).	
3.16 List and describe the functionality provided by Dreamweaver for XML.	
3.17 Given a coding tool or feature, describe the purpose of or how to use that tool or feature (tools or features include: Code and Design View, Code Collapse, Code Navigation, Code Hinting, Coding Context Menu option).	1–B
3.18 Discuss considerations related to naming conventions and case sensitivity (e.g., variations between UNIX and Windows).	2–B
3.19 Annotate files by using Design Notes and Comments.	
4.0 Managing and maintaining sites	
4.1 Manage collaboration with multiple developers by using Check In-Check Out.	
4.2 List and describe the different methods for accessing a remote site (methods include: FTP, LAN, VSS, WebDAV).	
4.3 Given an access method, configure site definitions.	2–A
4.4 Transfer and synchronize files to and from a remote server (options include: Cloaking, background file transfer, Get, Put).	
4.5 Manage assets, links, and files for a site.	
4.6 Configure preferences, and explain the process required to compare files.	
4.7 Validate a site prior to deployment (options include: link checking, accessibility checking, validating markup).	6–A

Lesson Labs

Due to classroom setup constraints, some labs cannot be keyed in sequence immediately following their associated lesson. Your instructor will tell you whether your labs can be practiced immediately following the lesson or whether they require separate setup from the main lesson content.

Lesson 1 Lab 1

Preparing to Use the Dreamweaver Environment

Data Files:

index.htm, enus_084204_01_solution.zip

Scenario:

You want to advertise your company's products through a website. You have decided to create it using the Dreamweaver application. Before proceeding with the work, you want to be thorough with the location and functionality of the various interface elements. Also, you want to modify the interface, so that the required tools can be accessed easily.

1. Launch the Dreamweaver application.

2. **What does the URL of a website consist of?**

3. From the *C:\084204Data\Getting Started with Dreamweaver\Everything for Coffee* folder, open the **index.htm** file.

4. On the **Insert** bar, select the various tabs to view their options.

5. Hide the **CSS** panel group.

6. Dock the **Application** panel group to the left of the document window.

7. Group the **Server Behaviors** panel (in the **Application** panel group) with the panels in the **Files** panel group.

8. Save the workspace layout as *Customized.*

Lesson 2 Lab 1

Building a Website

Data Files:

customer_service.htm, enus_084204_02_solution.zip

Before You Begin:

Choose **Window→Workspace Layout→Designer** to restore the Designer layout.

Scenario:

Having explored and customized the Dreamweaver environment, you are now ready to create the website. You decide to start by organizing the files required for creating the website, in a folder.

---

1. Define a new website with the name *Everything For Coffee* and set the **C:\084204Data\ Creating a Website\Everything for Coffee** folder as the local root folder.

---

2. Create a blank HTML document.

---

3. In the document, enter the text *Coffee Makers* and change its font type to **Arial, Helvetica, sans-serif,** paragraph format to **Heading 1,** font style to **Italic,** and color to **#CC9966.**

---

4. Save the web page as *coffee_makers.htm.*

---

5. In the **Files** panel, create a new folder with the name *Working.*

---

6. Move the **customer_service.htm** file into the **Working** folder.

Lesson 3 Lab 1

Adding Design Elements to a Web Page

Data Files:

cup.jpg, everything-for-coffee.jpg, customer-service.jpg, coffee_makers_home1.jpg, gourmet_beans_home1.jpg, coffee_filters_home1.jpg, cups_and_mugs_home1.jpg, history_of_coffee_home1.jpg

Before You Begin:

Define the Everything for Coffee site, using the data from the C:\084204Data\Adding Design Elements to Web Pages\Everything for Coffee folder.

Scenario:

You have started working on the home page of the Everything for Coffee site. The requirement for the home page is that it should be visually attractive.

---

1. In a new HTML document, create a table with 3 rows and 2 columns, and set the table width to **779.**

---

2. In the first two cells, in the first row, insert the **cup.jpg** image and the **everything-for-coffee.jpg** image, respectively, set the alternate text for both the images to *everything for coffee* and set the vertical alignment of the second cell to **Bottom.**

---

3. In the second row, set the background color of the first cell to *#88775B* and insert a table within it with 5 rows and 1 column and set the width as *241.*

---

4. Insert the **coffee_makers_home1.jpg, gourmet_beans_home1.jpg, coffee_filters_home1.jpg, cups_and_mugs_home1.jpg,** and **history_of_coffee_home1.jpg** images in each row of the table, and set the alternate text to *coffee makers, gourmet beans, coffee filters, cups and mugs, history of coffee,* respectively.

---

5. Set the horizontal alignment of each row of the nested table to **Center.**

---

6. In the second row, second cell, insert the **customer_service.jpg** image.

---

7. Merge the last row, set the background color to *#DCCCB2* and the horizontal alignment to **Center.**

---

8. In the merged row, insert a table with 1 row, 1 column and set the table width to *600.*

---

9. In the new table, type *Home I Trademarks I Copyrights I Privacy Policy I Terms & Conditions.*

---

10. Save the file as *index.html* and close it.

Lesson 4 Lab 1
Working with Links

Objective:
Work with links.

Data Files:
customer_service.html, coffee_makers.html

Before You Begin:
Define the Everything for Coffee site, using the data from the C:\084204Data\Working with Links\Everything for Coffee folder. If the Everything for Coffee site was previously defined in Dreamweaver, you must modify it so that it is based on the new data.

Scenario:
Your company's website contains a vast amount of information, and the visitors are finding it difficult to navigate through the site. You want the visitors to be able to easily access the home page and the customer service page from any page on the site. Also, since the coffee makers page is long, you want the visitors to be able to quickly move to the top of the page from any section.

1. Open the **customer_service.html** page.

2. At the bottom of the **customer_service.html** page, hyperlink the text **Home** for the **index.html** page.

3. Create an external hyperlink to the URL **http://www.ourglobalcompany.com/contactus.html** on the text **Click here.**

4. In the second paragraph, create an email link to the email address *support@everythingforcoffee.com* on the text **Support Services.**

5. Open the **coffee_makers.html** page and link the **Customer Service Center** image to the **customer_service.html** page.

6. On the everything_for_coffee_inner.jpg image, create a rectangular hotspot that covers the coffee cup image on the left and the text **Everything For Coffee** as well, and link it to the **index.html** page.

7. Create an anchor, called *top* for the **Coffee Makers** heading and link all instances of the text **Back to Top** to the anchor **#top.**

8. Save the web pages and preview it in Internet Explorer.

Lesson 5 Lab 1

Working with Frames

Data Files:

index.html, topmenu.html, sidemenu.html, content.html, everything-for-coffee-inner.jpg

Before You Begin:

Define the Everything for Coffee site, using the data from the C:\084204Data\Working with Frames\Everything for Coffee folder.

Scenario:

You want to have the company logo, the shopping cart, and the search box at the top, and the links to the copyright information and privacy policy at the bottom of all the pages on your website. You also want to vary the content on the other parts of a page depending on the link selected.

1. Create a **Fixed Top, Nested Left** frameset.

2. Specify the title attribute of **mainFrame** as *content,* **leftFrame** as *sidemenu,* and **topFrame** as *topmenu.*

3. Modify the frame name of **mainFrame** as *maincontent* and **leftFrame** as *sidemenu.*

4. Save the frameset as *coffeefilters.html.*

5. Link the **topFrame** to **topmenu.html,** the **sidemenu** frame to **sidemenu.html,** and the **maincontent** frame to **content.html.**

6. In the frameset, set the pixel value for **topFrame** to *150* and the pixel value of the **sidemenu** and **maincontent** frames to *200*

7. In the **topFrame,** link the **everything-for-coffee-inner.jpg** image to index.html and set the target to **_blank.**

8. In the **sidemenu** frame, select each link and set the target to the **maincontent** frame.

9. Save the web page and preview it in a browser.

Lesson 6 Lab 1

Uploading a Website

Data Files:

coffeefilters.html, cups_mugs.html

Before You Begin:

Define the Everything for Coffee site, using the data from the C:\084204Data\Uploading a Website\Everything for Coffee folder.

Scenario:

You have completed designing your website. Now, you want to check for broken links, target browser compatibility, validate site reports, and rectify errors before uploading it to your local site folder.

1. Check the site map and view the dependent files on the site.

2. Check for broken links, external links, and orphaned files for the entire current local site.

3. In the **index.html,** link the **Coffee Filters** image to the **coffeefilters.html** file.

4. Open the **cups_mugs.html** file and validate it.

5. Using the **Links** category of the **Page Properties** dialog box, set the color of the visited links to *#660000* and save the file.

6. Set the target browser as Internet Explorer 6.0, and check for browser compatibility.

7. Generate site reports for the **Missing Alt Text** option for the entire current local site.

8. Generate site reports for the entire current local site, with the associated **W3C/WCAG P.2 Accessibility** option disabled.

9. Save the site report as *myreport.xml.*

10. Edit the site definition by selecting **Local Network** as the remote access method.

11. Create a new folder named *Test Coffee* in the **C:\084204Data\Uploading a Website** folder and set it as the remote folder.

12. Upload the files to the **Test Coffee** folder, and in the expanded **Files** panel, view the site map.

Solutions

Lesson 1

Activity 1-1

1. **What does the first part of a URL indicate?**

   a) IP address

   b) Domain name

   c) File name

   ✓ d) Protocol

2. **Which statement is true about websites?**

   a) A website can contain only one web page.

   b) The web pages on a website cannot be linked through images.

   ✓ c) HTML can be used for creating web pages.

   d) Websites can contain information only in the form of text.

3. **True or False? Before creating a website, you need to identify the audience who will be visiting the site.**

   ✓ True

   ___ False

Activity 1-2

2. **Which component in the Dreamweaver interface provides information about the size and the magnification level of a document?**

   ✓ a) The status bar

   b) The Insert bar

   c) The Property Inspector

   d) The Document toolbar

4. **When would you use the Property Inspector?**

   a) To switch between the different views to view a document.

   b) To insert objects such as tables, graphics, spry widgets, and hyperlinks.

   c) To view the size of the current document.

   ✓ d) To modify the properties of objects such as text and graphics.

Lesson 1 Follow-up

Lesson 1 Lab 1

2. **What does the URL of a website consist of?**

   The URL of a website consists of the protocol that is used to access the website, and the IP address or the domain name of the website.

Lesson 4

Activity 4-2

3. **True or False? Email links can be created only for text.**

   ___ True

   ✓ False

Glossary

Adobe CSS Advisor
A website that provides information, suggestions, and tips on the latest browser and code issues in Dreamweaver.

anchor
A link that takes users to a particular location on a page.

Dreamweaver extensions
Software that can be added to the Dreamweaver application to enhance its capabilities.

Frames panel
Provides a visual representation of the organization of frames on a web page.

frames
Used to lay out a web page by dividing the browser window into multiple regions.

frameset
Used to store information about the layout and properties of a set of frames.

Get method
Used to copy files from a remote site to a local site.

GIF
(Graphic Interchange Format) A graphic file format that is limited to 256 colors and therefore, is most useful for images with few colors or with large areas of flat colors.

home page
The entry point of a website. It provides access to the other pages in the site.

hotspot
An area on an image, which can be clicked to open a linked web page.

HTML
(HyperText Markup Language) A scripting language that is used to create a web page.

Hyperlinks
Links that reference another web page on the same website or a different website.

image map
A single image that contains multiple hotspots, which can be clicked to open a linked web page.

JPEG
(Joint Photographic Experts Group) A graphic file format that uses compression to dramatically reduce the file size of the images, thus allowing for faster download and display.

list
Used to display content in a structured format.

Nested tables
Tables that are placed within a cell.

PNG
(Portable Network Graphic) A graphic file format that supports more than 256 colors along with transparency.

Put method
Used to upload files from a local site to a remote site.

Results panel
Contains tools that you can use to search for information and validate the web pages for accessibility and browser compatibility issues.

Site Definition wizard
A wizard that is used to define a website.

site map
A hierarchical visual representation of the structure of a website.

Tables
A structured format that allows you to present data in grids of rows and columns.

template
A document that contains predefined design elements, such as graphics and text. It can be used to create several web pages that share common design elements.

validator preferences
The settings that apply to the Dreamweaver validator.

web page
A document created using the HTML code.

website
A collection of web pages displayed on the Internet.

Index

A

anchor, 98

D

Dreamweaver extensions, 30

F

frames, 104
frameset, 105

G

GIF, 55

H

hotspot, 93
HTML, 3
Hyperlinks, 84

J

JPEG, 55

L

Lists, 34

M

maps
  image, 93

site, 134

N

Nested tables, 62

P

pages
  home, 29
  web, 2
panels
  Frames, 105
  Results, 123
PNG, 55

S

Site Definition wizard, 22

T

Tables, 60
template, 43

V

validator preferences, 124

W

website, 2